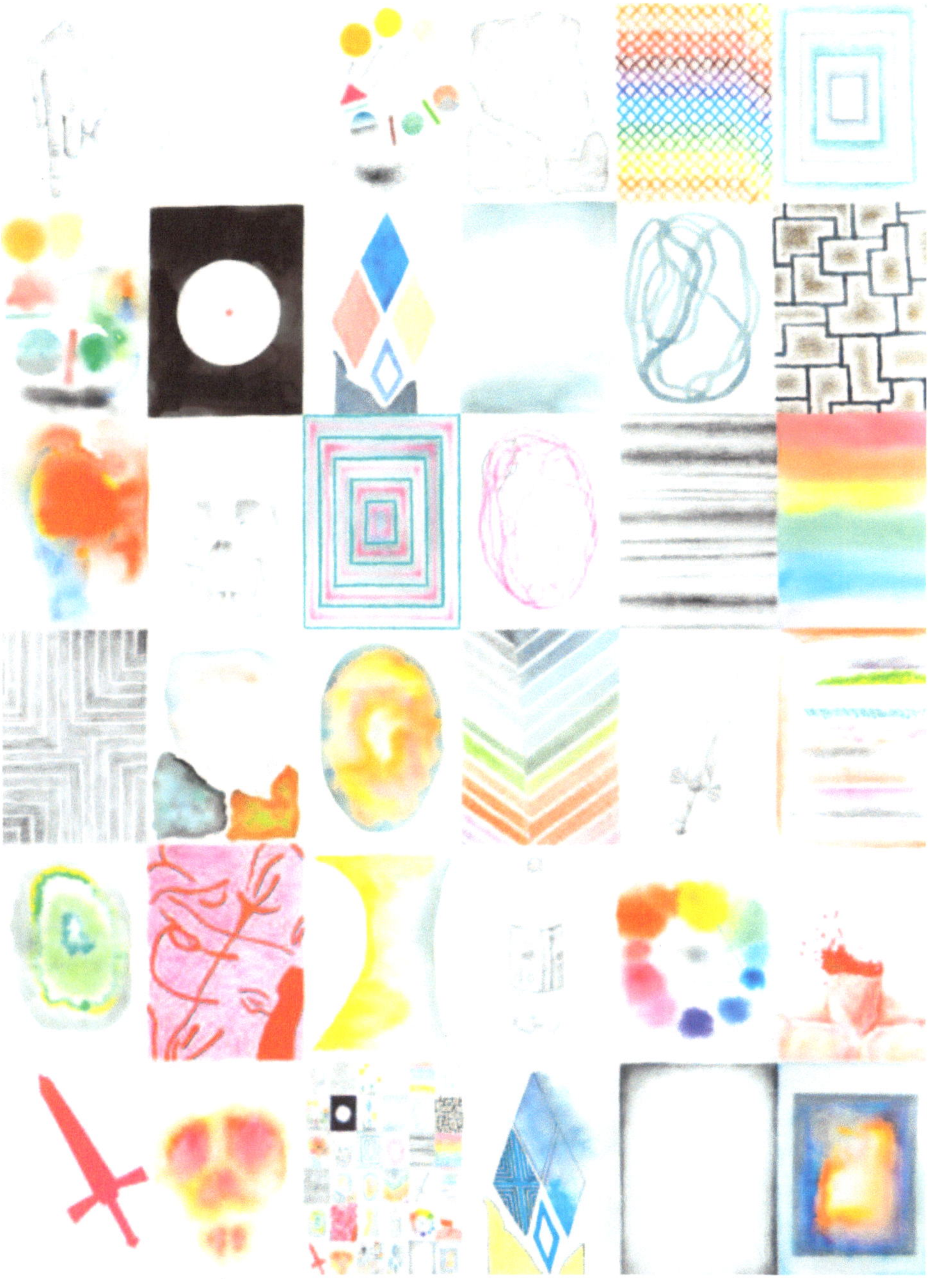

Finding, 2011

Casey Jex Smith

Wars and Rumors of Wars

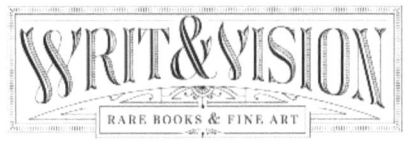

WRIT & VISION

RARE BOOKS & FINE ART

Writ & Vision

274 West Center Street

Provo, Utah 84601

801-647-7383

This catalogue accompanies the Writ & Vision gallery exhibition,
Casey Jex Smith: Wars and Rumors of Wars, curated by Glen Nelson,
October 2, 2015 through November 2, 2015

cover: Sisyphean Shards, 2014

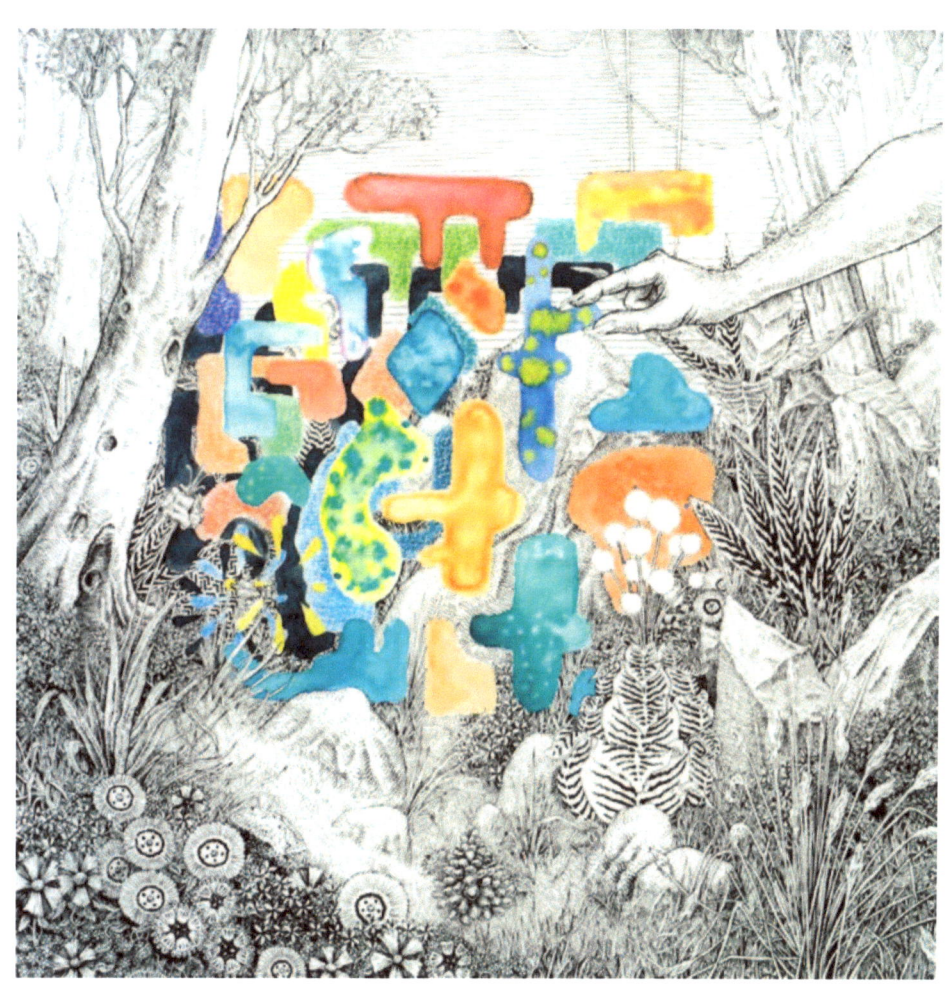

Pinch, 2015

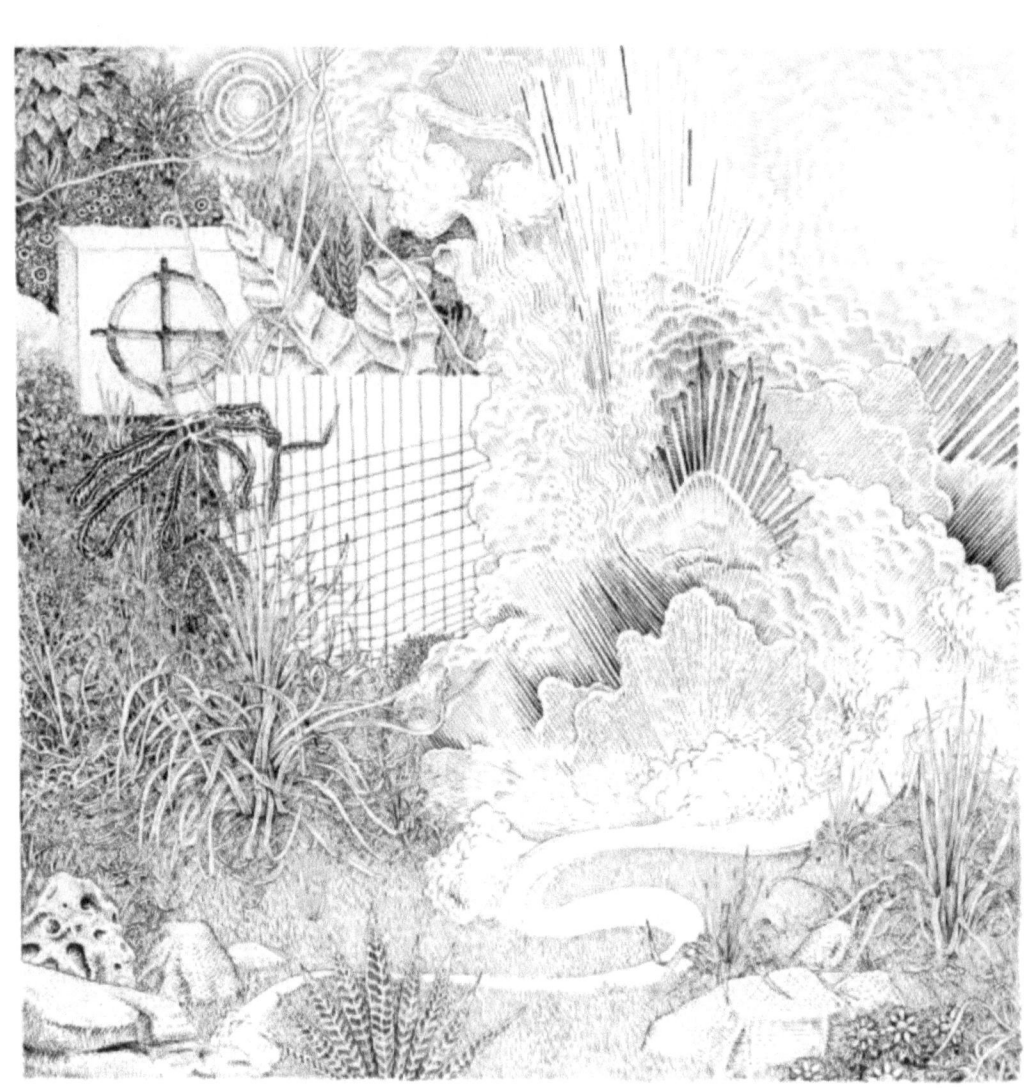

Vultures, 2014

Casey Jex Smith
Wars and Rumors of Wars

Glen Nelson

Introduction by Brad Kramer

Writ & Vision
Provo, Utah

Introduction

Brad Kramer

Writ & Vision

If the tension between play and competition—between free, unalloyed creativity and the ruthless pursuit of market success—is intrinsic to modern art itself (Warhol is often criticized/applauded for erasing the distinction between artistic and commercial production), it is rarely so vividly displayed as in the work of Casey Jex Smith. Not just in the artist's strife to produce work that is simultaneously imaginatively original and comparatively marketable but in the thematic content and composition itself. So much of Smith's work is joyfully creative, almost child-like, filled with the aesthetic wonder of a role-playing game or an epic fantasy novel, yet it consistently engages themes that are mature and deeply serious, from warfare to mythic and religious symbolism, themes that tap into the neural pathways where our most competitive impulses reside.

There is another tension that plays itself out in surprising ways in Smith's work on the purely formal or methodological plane: between drawing and painting. Smith is essentially a draftsman, and drawing is his dominant (a word that also implicates aggressive competition) creative form. Yet his work defies the reductive overtones that labeling him a draftsman implies, as if his work were somehow "limited" to drawing. If there is a general consensus in the art world that painting involves a depth, or complexity, or richness, or sheer gravity not possible with drawing, Smith's "drawings" utterly disregard that distinction. If Smiths' work can be "reduced" to something having to do with drawing, it is that he produces drawings with all of the largesse and force and density and intricacy of great paintings.

And here I'll revisit the comparison to Warhol. Not that Smith's works would ever strike either a casual or even a very adroit viewer as visibly

Warholesque, but that Smith, like Warhol (though in a very un-Warhol-like manner), so forcefully blurs the line between different ways of producing fine art as to cause us to question our basic assumptions that the difference ever mattered at all. This constant work of forcing us to reconsider what we thought we knew about art and the distinctions by which modern art defines and taxonomizes itself is something that, I think, Warhol would proudly claim as part of his legacy, even in the work of an artist who hails from the centers of Mormondom.

Provo, September 1, 2015

Playing at War

Glen Nelson

It's a surprisingly short evolution from a handful of military officers moving toy soldiers across a tabletop battlefield in 1812 to the estimated 71 million people who watched video gaming eSports played in arenas last year. Further, the battle impulse of play (and the playfulness of battle) has never been stronger than it is right now.

This kind of gaming is quite distinct from board games, card games, and chess—many of which also sprang from the narrative of the battlefield. Players moving pieces on a chessboard, for example, never pretend that they are a knight or a queen. They never articulate by what weapon a piece is captured, simply that it is taken. The more immersive the battle play, the more it is connected to role-play.

Modern games of war started with tin soldiers. Georg Leopold von Reiswitz, a lieutenant in the Prussian army, and his son wrote a manual for military gaming in 1812 called *Instructions for the Representation of Tactical Maneuvers under the Guise of a Wargame*. In this *kriegsspiel* (German for "war play"), the field of play was marked off as a grid on a tabletop, and using toy figures and dice, opposing armies of red and blue moved, strategized, and battled each other, overseen by an umpire. But the rules were complex and a game took forever—longer, some complained, than the actual battles they sought to simulate.

It was the father of science fiction, H. G. Wells—author of *The Time Machine*, *The Island of Doctor Moreau*, and *The War of the Worlds*—who made battle games fun. In 1913, Wells wrote a delightful, short book, *Little Wars: A Game for Boys from twelve years of age to one hundred and fifty and for that more intelligent sort of girl who likes boy's games and books*.

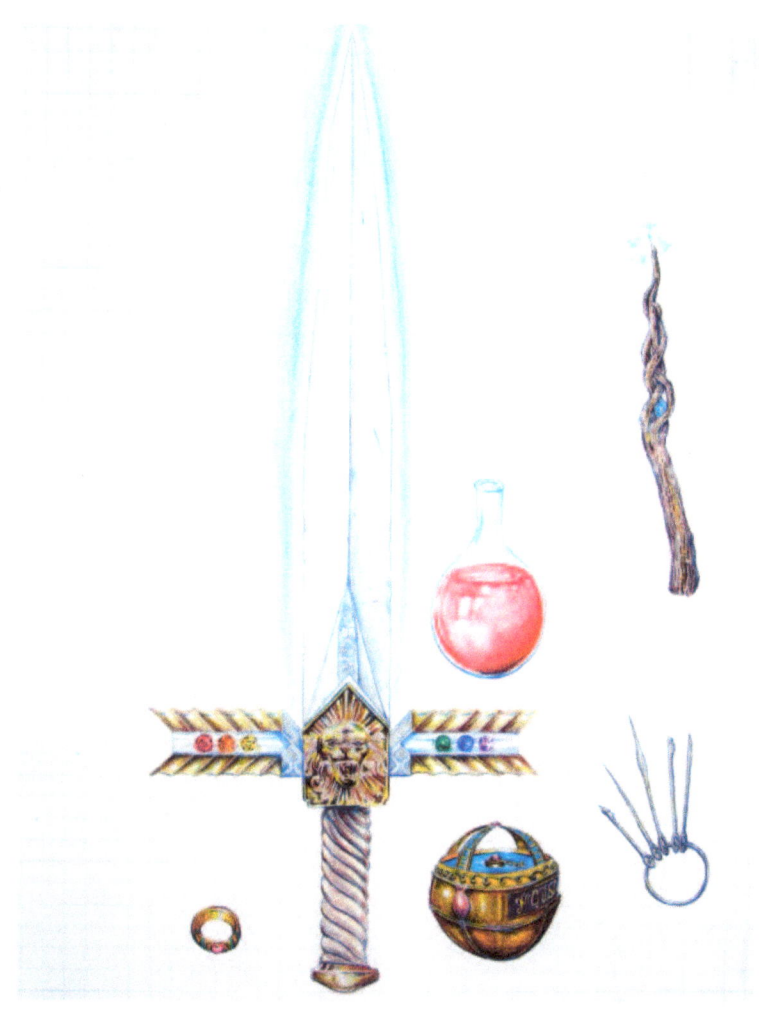

Sword of Laban +5 and Gear, 2010

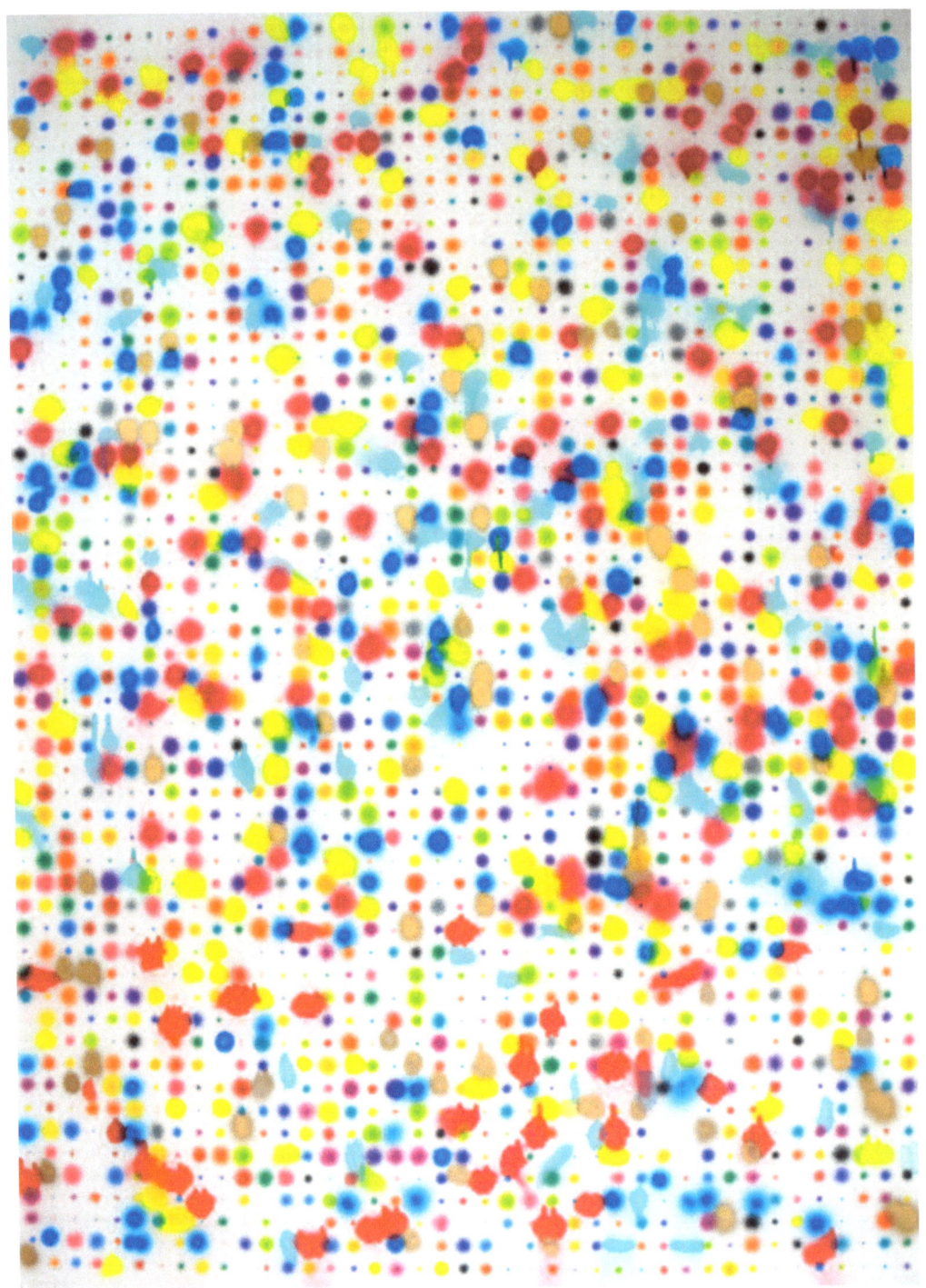

Too Many Attacks to Count, 2012

His goal was to create a battle game using tin infantry, cavalry, artillery, and model houses, orchards, rivers, meadows, forests, and hills. The game became possible because of the invention late in the 19th century of the spring breechloader gun. This 4.7" weapon shot little wooden pegs about one inch long with great accuracy, "capable of hitting a toy soldier nine times out of ten at a distance of nine yards," Wells wrote. He called the gun a "priceless gift to boyhood."

Little Wars is a memoir that narrates the creation, development, rules, and play of Wells' game. It specifies how many inches players can move on a turn, how long the deliberation can last, how to calculate melees between opposing forces, and numerous other rules regarding the taking of prisoners, the manning of guns, how terrain is navigated, how to retreat and advance, when guns can be used and when not, and so forth.

Another of his innovations was moving the game out into the open air. Wells took photographs of himself playing an extended game on the lawn with 2" tall soldiers, amid equally scaled trees, houses, markets, castles, and mountains. *Little Wars*, like many other role-playing games, is a rulebook, essentially. Players found their own soldiers and other game pieces or they created them all by themselves. There was craft involved and creativity and preparation.

For a century, this game spawned numerous others. At the same time, toy trains and other miniature marvels became fixations for children's play. A naval war game, to give an example, included a rulebook, one ship, a string to measure distance, and a protractor—so the players could calculate wind velocity, sailing speeds, and other variables in sea battles. These were games, but they weren't mindless games.

A curious thing happened to war gaming after mid-century. The success—or should we just call it an obsession?—of J. R. R. Tolkiens's fantasy books, *The Hobbit* (1937) and *The Lord of the Rings* (1937-1949) began to alter what battle play could be like. To the cast of generals and sergeants, sabers and canons, game creators added wizards and dragons, special powers and spells.

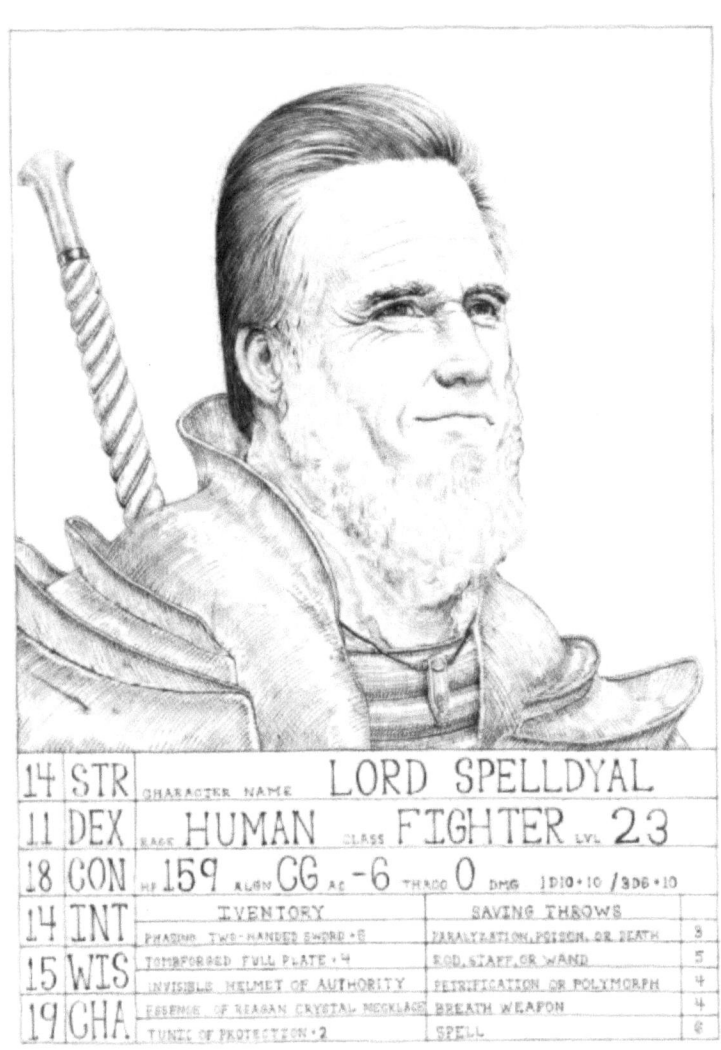

Lord Spelldyal, 2012

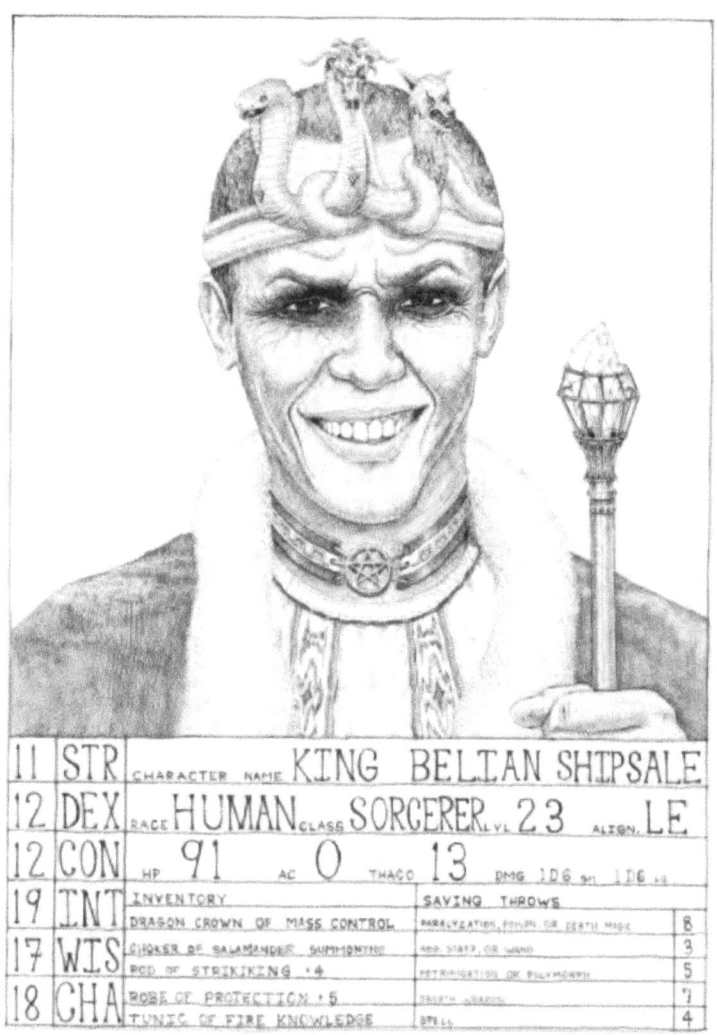

11	STR	CHARACTER NAME	KING BELIAN SHIPSALE		
12	DEX	RACE HUMAN CLASS SORCERER LVL 23 ALIGN. LE			
12	CON	HP 91 AC 0 THAC0 13 DMG 1D6 9H 1D6 +3			
19	INT	INVENTORY	SAVING THROWS		
		DRAGON CROWN OF MASS CONTROL	PARALYZATION, POISON OR DEATH MAGIC	8	
17	WIS	CHOKER OF SALAMANDER SUMMONING	ROD, STAFF, OR WAND	3	
		ROD OF STRIKING +4	PETRIFICATION OR POLYMORPH	5	
18	CHA	ROBE OF PROTECTION +5	BREATH WEAPON	7	
		TUNIC OF FIRE KNOWLEDGE	SPELL	4	

King Belian Shipsale, 2012

In the 1960s, gaming magazines, societies, and clubs promoted a number of new war games such as *Siege of Bodenburg* and *Battle of Arsuf*. *Chainmail* was the name of the 1971 game by Gary Gygax that combined medieval war games and Tolkien-influenced fantasy. This sent kids rushing to their toy boxes to see what creatures they already owned that could be reconfigured as game pieces for war. *Dungeons and Dragons* made its appearance in 1974. Drawing directly from *Chainmail* and adapted by Dave Arneson, this became a phenomenon and launched role-playing games into common vernacular.

But for adults who didn't know about such things, fantasy games sounded weird, even malevolent. What were the kids doing for hours down in the basement, rolling strange polyhedral dice and sometimes wearing costumes anyway, parents asked.

They should have gone downstairs and watched. It was not anarchy but its opposite: play revolving around strict rules of conduct. A 1981 novel and 1982 made-for-TV movie villified role-playing games, but they were exaggerated and salacious fictions. In real life, here were kids doing what they've done for centuries—battling, strategizing, and creatively pitting forces against each other. And unlike the prepackaged, scripted play of board games, role-playing games invited the players to be imaginative, to create the game piece figures, paint them, and build fanciful environments on which to play. It was DIY gaming. Many generations of related games followed—most of these consisted of illustrated rulebooks and figurines, sold separately.

As everybody knows, all of this changed with the computer.

Maybe not with *Pong* and *Space Invaders*, but in relatively short order, multi-player computer games, online games, and team-based war games proliferated, including *Defense of the Ancients* (2003), *World of Warcraft* (2004); *League of Legends* (2006), and *Minecraft* (2009). Of course, there are innumerable games now; the above titles are but a tiny sample. What is the difference between a South Korean teenage boy in 2015 building his own computer landscape for Minecraft and a British teenage boy in 1915 shooting wooden pegs at the enemy troop in *Little Wars*? Ultimately, not very much.

The global market for computer games is $91.5 billion today, according to "2015 Global Games Market Report." *World of Warcraft* has grossed over $10 billion, alone. Universities now offer athletic scholarships to eSport gamers who play in front of area stadiums full of fans. And gaming teams train like Olympians in highly competitive, globally broadcast tournaments. 40,000 people showed up to watch the live World Championship final battle in *League of Legends* last year—the winning team took home a trophy and a $1 million prize. Twitch.tv, a streaming platform recently acquired by Amazon.com, allows viewers to watch videos of other people playing computer games; it averages 100 million viewers a month.

That's not to say that adults love (and/or understand) the above. Name a generation that *hasn't* said that the next generation was wasting its time and should curtail its hours at play. As it has always been, work/play is an issue of balance. Parents hate their kids' music, and unless they've played the same games, they sort of hate their kids' games too.

Who decides that one kind of play is good and another bad? (A generation of athletes is finding out that taking all those hits to the head out on the field wasn't so healthy, after all.) Ultimately it comes down to an innate impulse to play, and increasingly in this wired world, to play remotely. Role-playing games have that ability in spades, now connected by the internet around the globe.

What does all this have to do with the art of Casey Jex Smith? Nothing and everything. He's a self-described gamer, and in interviews since the beginning of his career, he's talked about how his work resides in the intersection of computer games, Mormon symbols and ritual, and fine art history. Looking at his recent works, in particular, it is easy to imagine them as tableaux awaiting some game to begin (or its aftermath). Ogres and monsters populate them alongside Book of Mormon narratives, contemporary prophets, and celebrities who are rebranded as gaming characters.

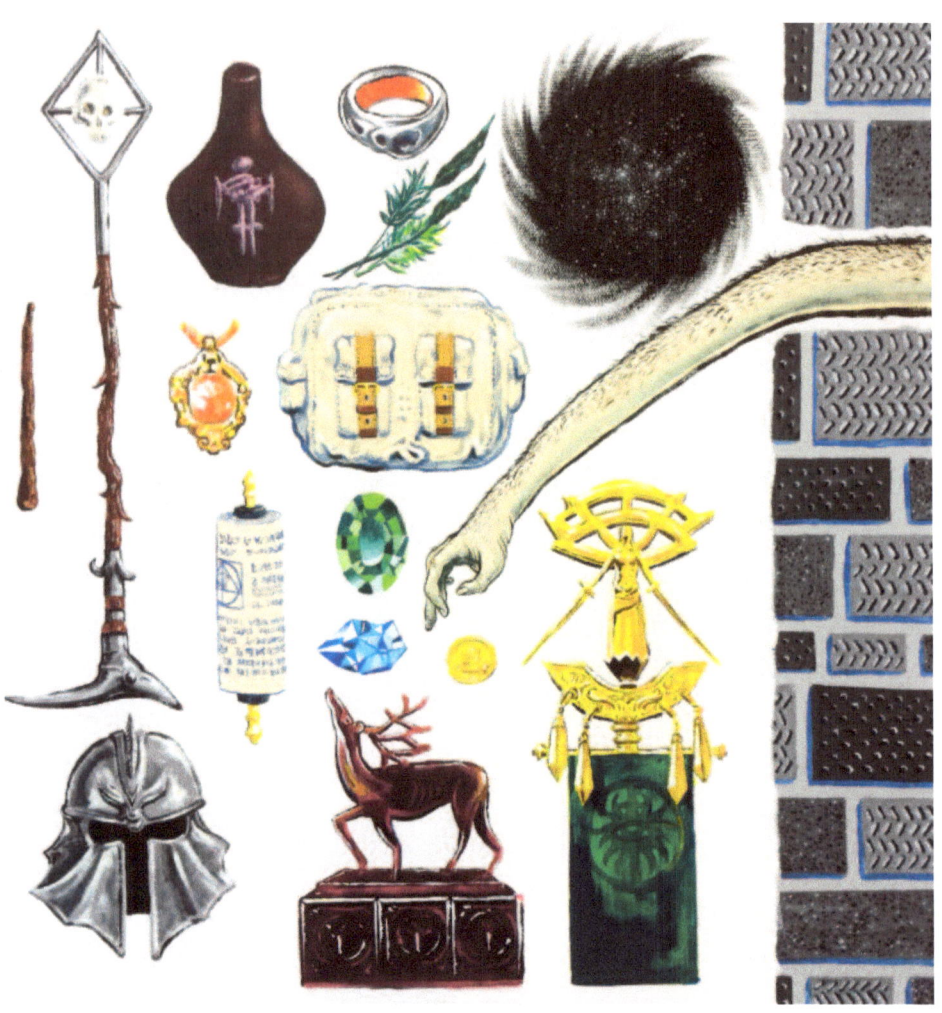

Stash, 2015

Are they war games settings, specifically? He has referred to the drawings as "power simulations." Recently, Smith has added colorful, abstract fine art works into the scenes, perhaps the spoils of war.

Smith's art is full of symbol and myth, but more than anything else, the paintings and drawings are allegorical worlds of joyful, youthful creativity. Viewers of these works become players in a game, and decoding the works, its own kind of battle. The artworks are artifacts of little wars. Just like role-playing games, they are fun, but they have point, too, if we take the time to consider their metaphors. This is not about darkness and violence—quite the opposite.

Ironically, H. G. Wells, the author of a game that popularized warfare as child's play, was a stanch Pacifist. He ends *Little War* with this thought, written only one year before the beginning of World War I:

You have only to play at Little Wars three or four times to realise just what a blundering thing Great War must be. Great War is at present, I am convinced, not only the most expensive game in the universe, but it is a game out of all proportion. Not only are the masses of men and material and suffering and inconvenience too monstrously big for reason, but—the available heads we have for it, are too small. That, I think, is the most pacific realisation conceivable, and Little War brings you to it as nothing else but Great War can do."

New York City, August 28, 2015

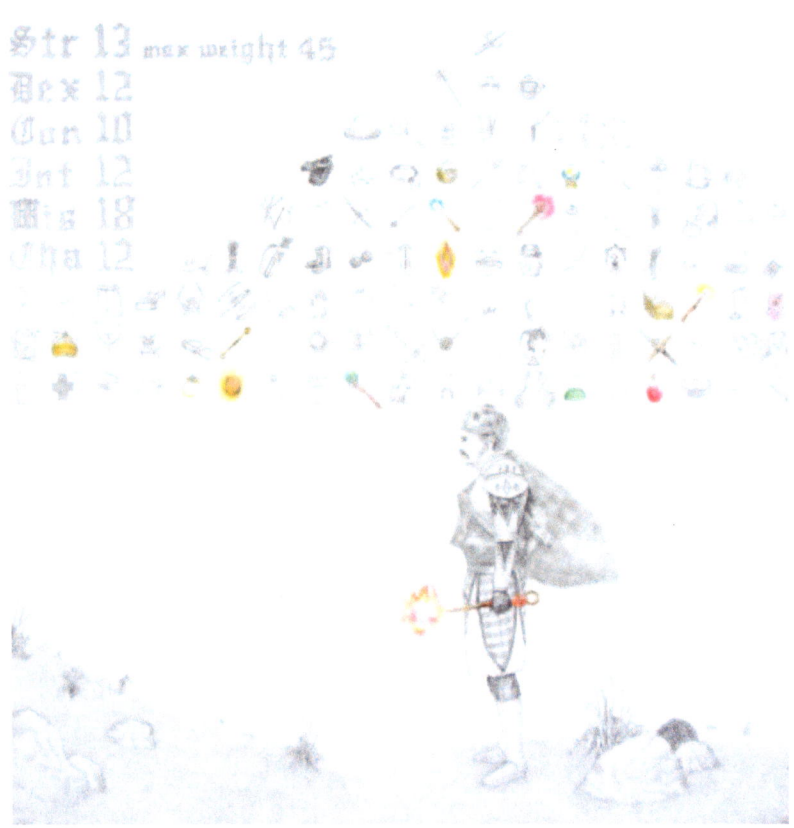

Str 13 max weight 45
Dex 12
Con 10
Int 12
Wis 18
Cha 12

Encumbered, 2010

Drawing Details

Casey Jex Smith and Glen Nelson

[interview conducted August 29-September 1, 2015]

Glen: Hi Casey. Let's get started.

Maybe I'm wrong, but the man in "Encumbered" looks like you. Is it a self-portrait, and what are all those objects above your head?

Casey: It is a self-portrait. You can tell by the gut sticking out. "Encumbered" refers to RPG video games [role-playing game] when your character is carrying too much gear in their backpack and cannot move. In the drawing I have illustrated real objects that we had in our house after having a baby. I felt overwhelmed by the looming responsibility of becoming the lone breadwinner in the family.

Glen: Let's take one of the drawings in the show and look at it closely. How about "Sisyphean Shards"?

Casey: Sure.

Glen: I assume that you're alluding to the legend of Sisyphus, the sad sack, perpetual boulder pusher. But why "Shards"?

Casey: Well, shards refer to magic crystals that a player in the XBox One game, *Dragon Age: Inquisition* finds during their adventure. When you have found enough shards, you can open a magically sealed door. Behind the door you find treasure, weapons, armor, etc. After each door, there is another door that opens into another room. And each successive door requires more shards to open it.

Being the obsessive player that I am, I feel the need to acquire every piece of loot that the game has to offer. I was three shards away from opening the last door when the game decided to make those last three disappear. I waited for months to see if it would get fixed in a patch, but the patch never came and I never got the satisfaction of opening that last, virtual door.

This drawing refers to that process of being on a never-ending quest

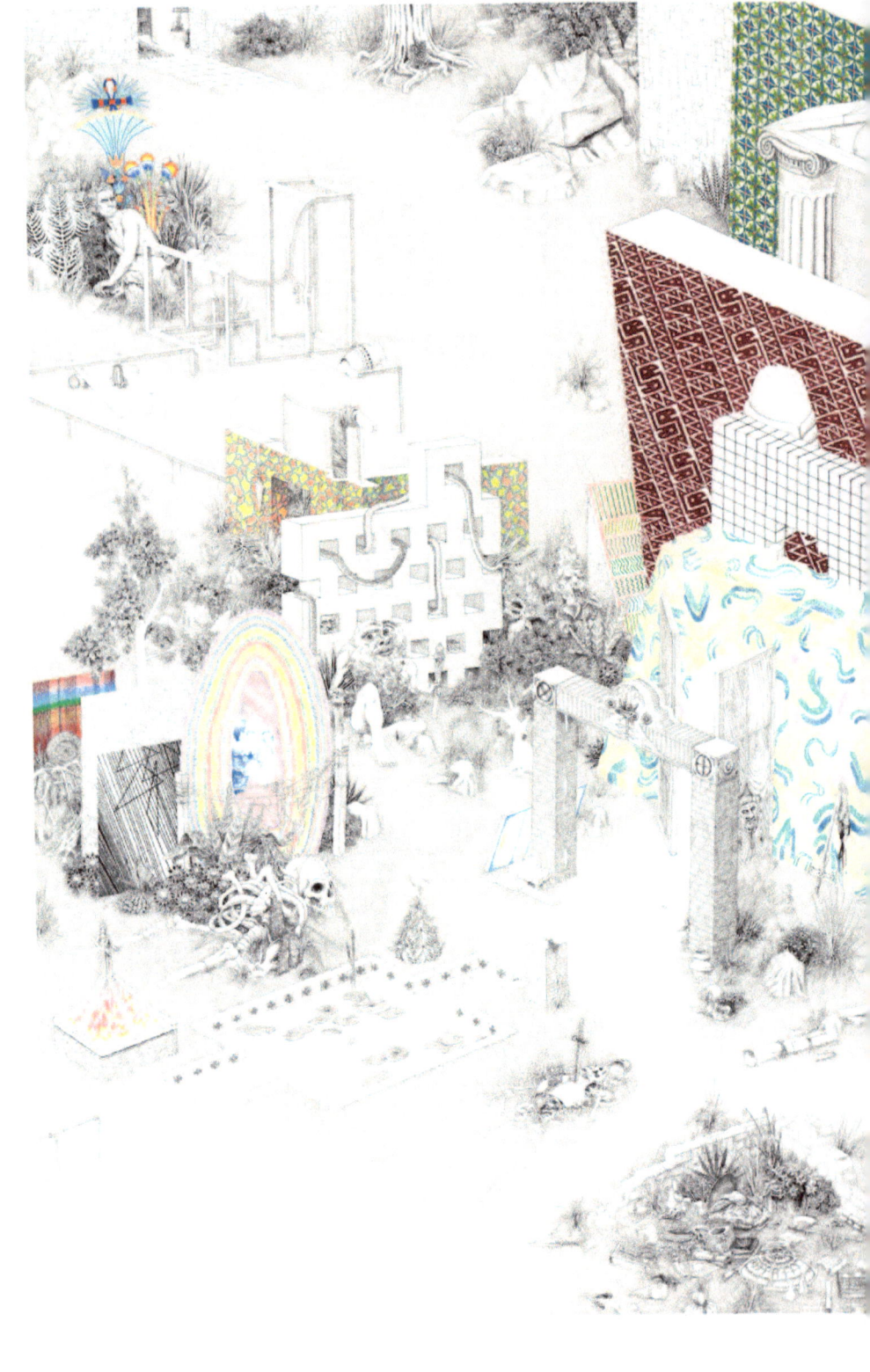

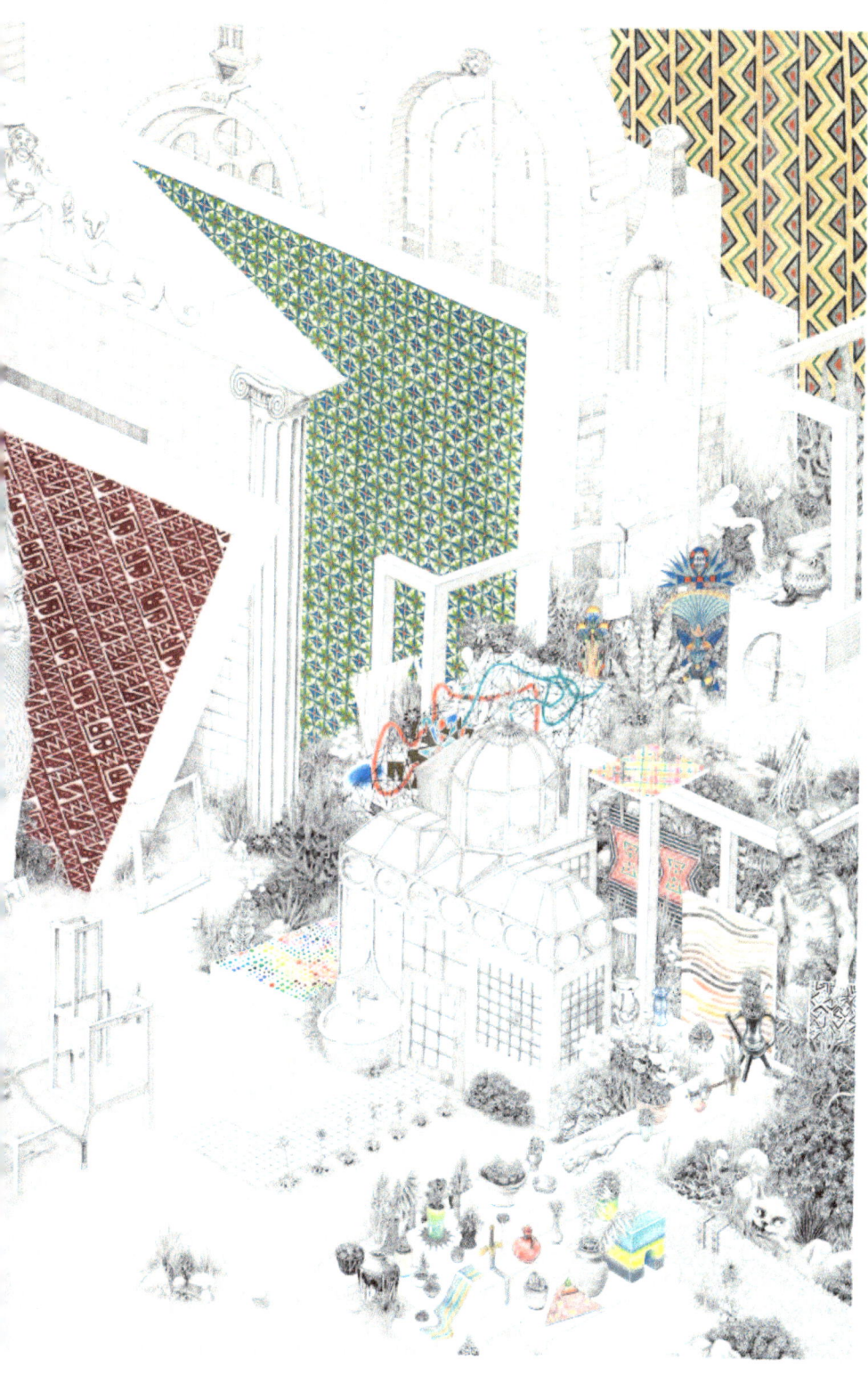

Sisyphean Shards, 2014

to open doors. The character goes on a quest, finds the right key, the answer to a riddle, the correct quest item to appease the Gods, and opens each door only to find another. Or maybe it's about washing dishes.

Glen: Sure. Gaming is a metaphor. There's so much going on in the drawing—and all of your works are like this—a lot of visual territory to cover (and uncover). I'm going to ask you about a few things that I see. You tell me why they're in the picture. Okay?

Casey: Cool. I warn you that not everything refers to something profound.

Glen: Feel free to make up stuff, then. There are many botanical drawings in here. Tell me about the colorful plants on the far left and far right margins with the fan and cross shapes, and about vegetation in general.

Casey: I love to put geometric abstraction butting up against organic material. And usually I keep them separate. But on those flowers I wanted to have an abstracted and flattened plant and combine the two. I came across an Egyptian textile that had this flower that was the perfect combination. Most of the time, I don't use any reference material when drawing my vegetation. I let myself make up plants. But because my imagination is limited, I end up with a vocabulary of something like ten plants that I just repeat. Hopefully in that way it looks like my landscape and not someone else's—another arbitrary rule that I created as justification.

Glen: I see three skeletons. One is a jumble of bones at the far right of the picture, one is impaled by a sword in the center of the drawing, and another on the left side of the pool. Now that's a crazy-looking beast. What is it?

Casey: Hopefully it's something so grotesque that it came out of John Carpenter's *The Thing*.

Glen: Can you examine for me the objects in the bottom center of the drawing? There are books, scrolls, papers, maps and weapons….

Casey: That's a pile of discarded quest items, broken weapons, rusted armor, and used foodstuffs, discarded after each adventure. I was thinking about the garbage piling up on Mount Everest.

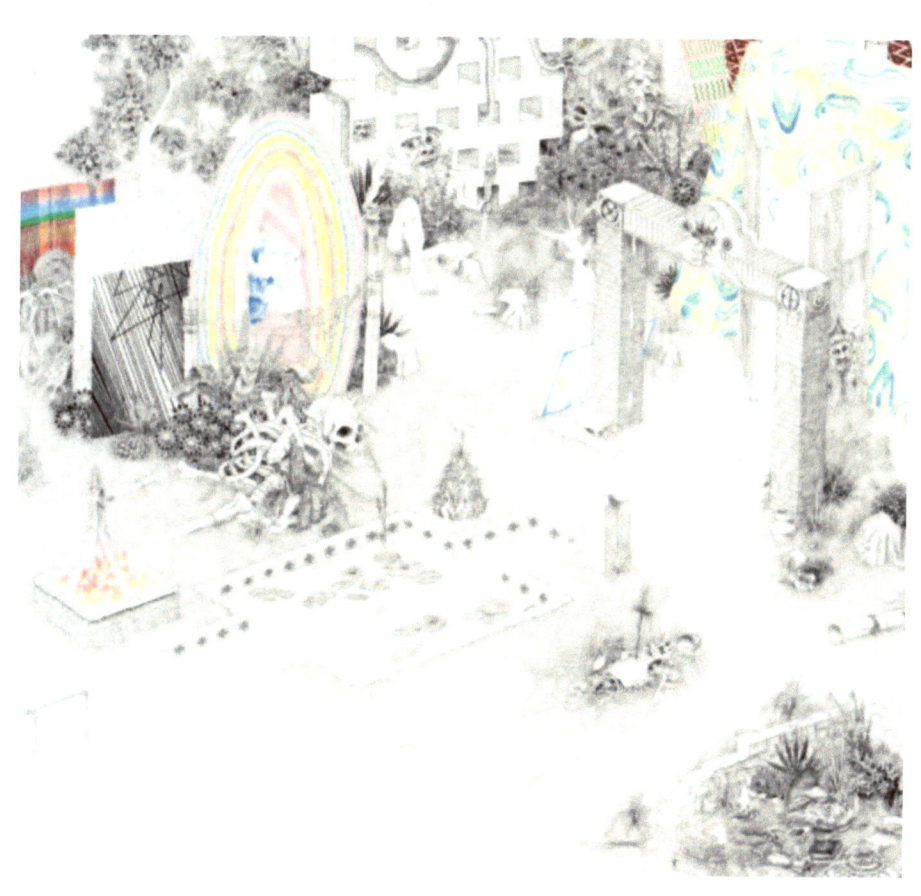

Sisyphean Shards (detail), 2014

Glen: Each quadrant of the drawings has its own creatures in it: a man in the left who looks to me like an angry Thomas Jefferson; a bearded guy with a scepter leaning against the wall; an old man on the far right side holding a painting; a crazed cat and some kind of lizard on the bottom right. Who or what are they, and why are they in the picture?

Casey: Ha-ha. That Thomas Jefferson fellow is a sculpture by Bernini of David—a David who was supremely confident, fit, and was ready and willing to change history. The lizard came from my three-year old daughter at the time obsessed with lizards. I read a lot lizard books. And the iguana seems to have the most texture on it of any lizard. So basically, he's there as a foil to the smooth, white pedestal he's basking on.

Glen: My apologies to Bernini and Jefferson. Tell me about the paintings placed in "Sisyphean Shards." The more I look, I see them everywhere, scattered around, leaning against other things. Tell me about them.

Casey: I love abstract painting. I love watching it trending in the art market. I love hearing about "Zombie Abstraction" and "Crapstraction" getting reamed in the press. In my drawings, they are useless distractions, kind of like video games. But the power they have in NY is immense. It might be my envy of the New Yorker, male, macho painter who makes a 12-foot canvas painting per week and can sell them for six figures a pop.

Glen: Aside from the money, I imagine that finishing a huge painting in a week would be very attractive to you, as a father of young children. How many hours did you spend drawing "Sisyphean Shards"?

Casey: I spent 8 months on "Sisyphean Shards." Now that's probably spending, on average, an hour a day because of teaching and other responsibilities. So probably about 200-250 hours.

Glen: There are some elements in the drawing that appear in other works hanging in the exhibition. Are these recurring characters and objects of special significance for you?

Casey: Yes. One of them is the limp sword.

Glen: I have to ask you about the armature in the shape of Utah, just right of center in the foreground.

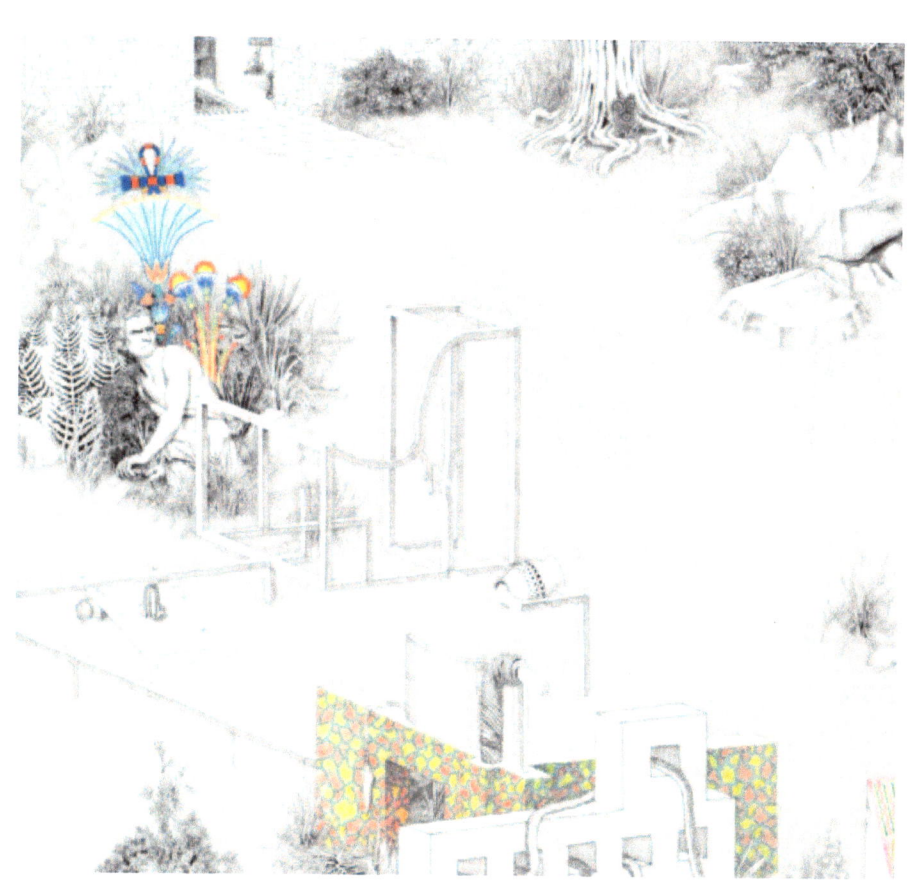

Sisyphean Shards (detail), 2014

Casey: Totally Sol Lewitt, Utah, ball & chain, and something Joseph Smith might have used to divine the location of water: a perfect formal mash of my identity.

Glen: Each of the increasingly large center doorways quotes a different culture. Tell me about them.

Casey: So there are recognizable references to Art History and there are patterns that are difficult to place. But these patterns were passed down from cultures where they had meaning and were likely used in some type of ritualistic practice. The last pattern was taken from a rug while I was watching *Twin Peaks*. And that pattern was likely appropriated from a Northwestern Native American tribe and modified for mass consumption. I feel like contemporary abstraction is a seven-degree-separation from a Peruvian funerary textile pattern, stripped of meaning.

Glen: What's going on in the far right of the picture? Is it some kind of treasury or greenhouse? Again, with so many abstract paintings.

Casey: Driving around in rural Ohio, I once saw an old farmhouse with an addition that had a glass domed, greenhouse-type structure. I think of it as housing some kind of benevolent NPC [non-player character] that creates potions for your quests, if you have given them the quest item they had asked for, which was probably the roots to some rare herb only found growing in the dung of a bog troll.

Glen: I don't know what to make of the large, colorful oval object at the far left. Is it a portal?

Casey: Right. Portals are always left in videogames in the right places so you don't have to retread the same path too many times. That becomes tedious and you can lose a player's interest.

Glen: Way at the top corner on the left, it looks like you've drawn an entrance to another space, maybe a domestic space. Where is it going?

Casey: It's temptation for the quest-weary. You can retire there. Once you discover that the doors never end, why keep trying?

Glen: I don't want to pour over every element of "Sisyphean Shards" and have you decode it—that would rob the viewers of fun. But I have one

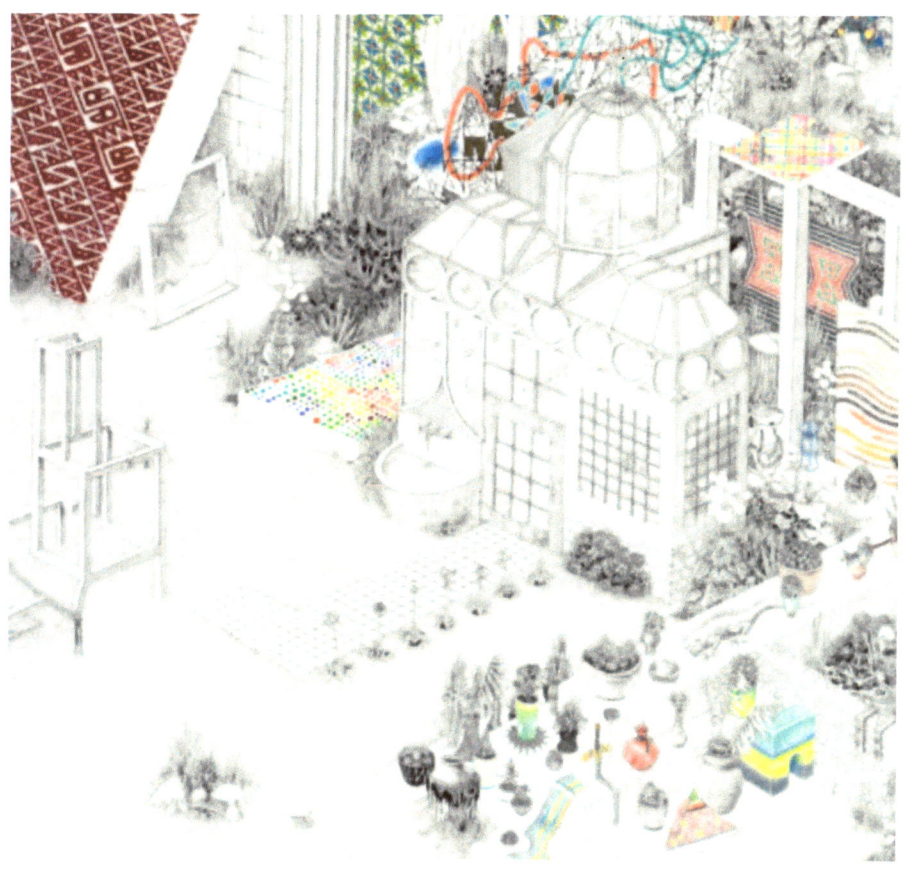

Sisyphean Shards (detail), 2014

more question about the drawing. I've noticed in this drawing and in a number of your other drawings that you quote directly from the artworks of your friends— Ryan Browning, Allan Ludwig, Jared Lindsay Clark, Daniel Everett, and Todd Chilton, among others. And I've seen them put elements of your drawing in their work, too. What's that about?

Casey: They are influences. I care more about their work than anyone else's. So what they paint or sculpt floats around in my mind. Sometimes it comes out as a conscious nod to their influence, and sometimes it's a subconscious decision because my creativity has a limit. I try to be aware when that happens, but artists just regurgitate what we consume and try and arrange it into something newish and meaningful, and hopefully not too derivative of another artist, especially someone living…, especially someone I went to school with at BYU.

Glen: We could go on labeling the numerous components of the image all day. And I guess that you could mound up responses higher and higher to explain every single mark, potentially—why you made the color choices you did, or why a blade of grass bends to the left instead of the right, or any number of artistic decisions, large and small. But let me approach it another way. Games are full of rules. Your pictures give the impression that you are engaged in a kind of role play as you create a picture. Is that fair to say? What are your rules in picture-making? I can think of one: you have to stay within the confines of the paper's edges. What else?

Casey: As an artist you do have to create self-imposed rules that apply to an inner logic. For a few years, I had a rule that when I make ink drawings, that lines mustn't touch. They had to run parallel. No cross-hatching. This had something to do with the viewer being able to see every line and therefore understand completely its construction. If I was building up value, it would be done with line proximity. What I ended up with were drawings that had very light values that had to be seen in person to understand—probably a terrible career decision when the art world was moving to the internet and every award, scholarship, residency, was judged according to small jpeg images. I'm still fighting against myself to push values darker.

 After 2008, I made a new rule to file the entire picture plane. Before, I was trying to break from traditional religious illustration and only render parts that were important and try to forget about creating illusionary space.

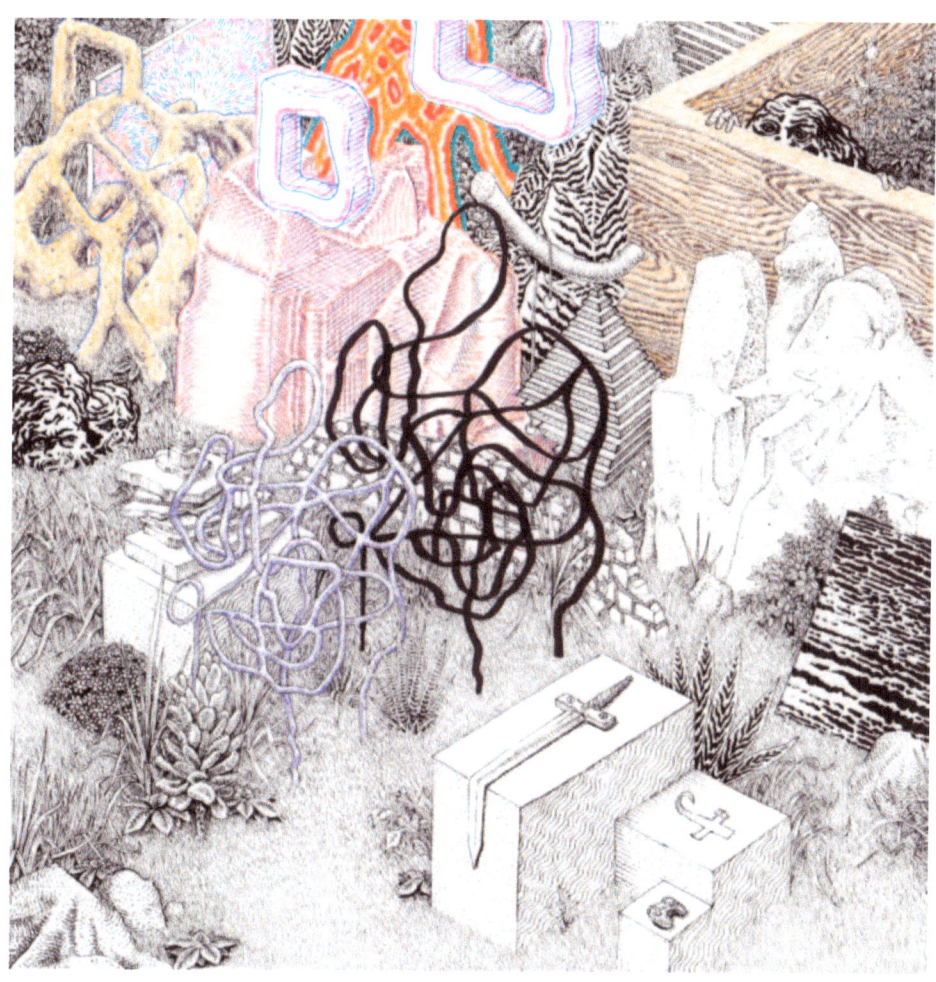

Limp, 2015

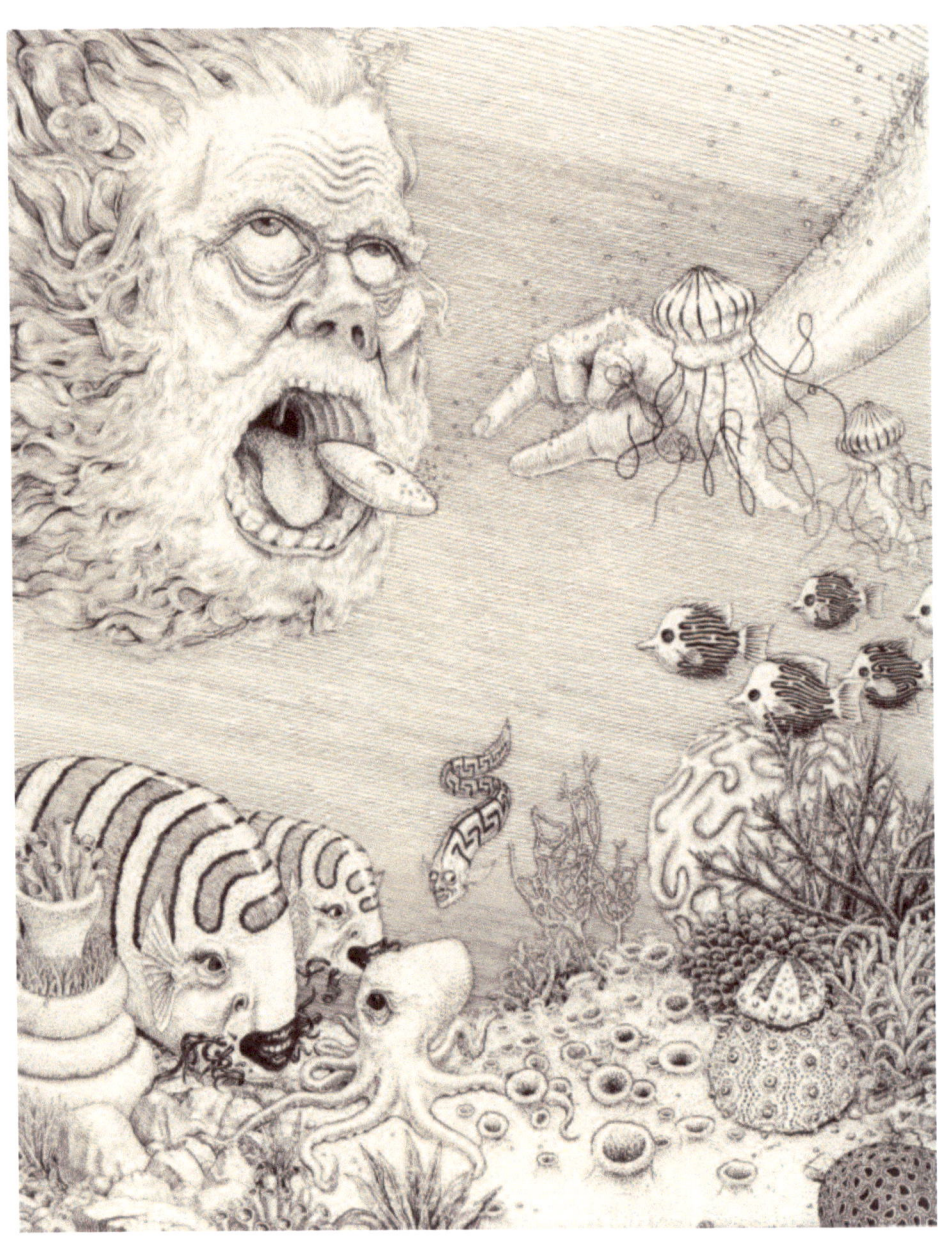

Like Unto a Dish, 2013

One more rule is I get to eat and drink whatever I want when I'm making work in the studio. No limit on soda or junk food.

Glen: You have used the phrase "power simulations" to describe your drawings. I suspect that you're talking about something more than depicting scenes where power is on display.

Casey: There are very few things in life that I feel I have total control over. Art and video games are the two places where I can feel powerful and where I feel my voice can be fully heard. I recently spoke my mind at my place of employment and was nearly let go. When I am in the studio I can speak the truth without repercussions.

Glen: I've had a couple of illuminating experiences watching other people look at your pictures. One took place in New York at the Drawing Center in 2008. I walked into the gallery and saw your drawing of Abinadi, straight out of the Freiberg Book of Mormon, except that you retained King Noah and the leopards and replaced Abinadi with an abstraction. The other people in the gallery didn't know anything about Mormonism. They were intrigued by the power of the image although they couldn't articulate why.

Another experience was almost the opposite. Some friends of mine came to my apartment and saw a drawing that you did in 2009 of President Monson recast as a fantasy hero, "Thorgar Serpenthelm Greatsoul." It's similar to the three images in this exhibition that describe the character's powers, class, weapons, etc. These friends are Mormon, but I didn't know how they would react. At first, they just looked, and when they recognized who it was, they smiled at the novelty of it. After I explained the philosophy behind the drawing very briefly, though, they fell in love with it. To them, it spoke to their deep feelings for him, but in an entirely original and respectful way.

That's a long set up for this question: quotations from LDS illustrations in Contemporary Art can come off derisively, but I don't get that tone from your work. What power do you find in images that only Mormons are likely to be able to discern, the Nauvoo Temple sunstone redefined as Cyclops in "Churning," for example?

Casey: Dungeons & Dragons is a language and Mormon iconography is a language. And when you speak both, you derive meaning through the lens of both, like a pair of glasses with different prescriptions in each lens; but you see one image. That's what happens to something like the Sunstone. He is the guardian of the Nauvoo temple and portals to other dimensions. So when people are looking at your work, it helps if they speak your languages. And I think that's where I've run into some trouble with accessibility, sometimes. Luckily those aren't the only two languages I use, but the work that has had the least success commercially leans more towards those two languages and relies less on art history, although it's probably the work that is the most original.

Glen: On August 4, 2015, the LDS Church announced a new volume of *Joseph Smith papers, Revelations and Translations, Volume 3: Printer's Manuscript of the Book of Mormon*. The book also includes four photographs of a seer stone and its cloth bag, which the Church said was likely used by Joseph Smith in the process of translation. What was your first impression of the news and the photographs?

Casey: I had heard about the stone, but didn't know that it existed. And when I saw the image I was struck by how pretty it was. And immediately I knew it had to be in a drawing and be part of a possible series of seer stones. They are most certainly magical objects of a high level. And I'll just add it to the collection of magic items in scripture. It belongs. We are a magical church.

Glen: A few works in the exhibition have a formal structure of the grid. The elements are presented as a grid themselves, or they have a drawn grid underneath them. I'm thinking of "Sword of Laban +5 and Gear," "Too Many Attacks to Count," "142 Painting Studies or Pries Spells," "Finding Patterns," "Seer Stone," and "Stash." And in other works you've drawn a simple grid as a part of the image. Given role-playing gaming history's reliance on the grid as a battlefield foundation, are you making a stronger connection in your works to gaming as a structure, or are you making reference to Minimalist art and its love of the grid?

Casey: I am referencing Minimalism's reliance on the grid, map-making in Dungeons & Dragons, the gridded backpack items in *Baldur's Gate*, and the 21st Century visual tool of organizing images either in an image search or an archive like Pinterest. The grid organizes. It democratizes. It designs. It makes sense out of chaos. It provides structure to the structureless. Everybody needs the grid!

Glen: I am curious about the largest drawing in the exhibition, "Lehi's Vision." I assume it alludes to the Book of Mormon scripture in which Lehi has

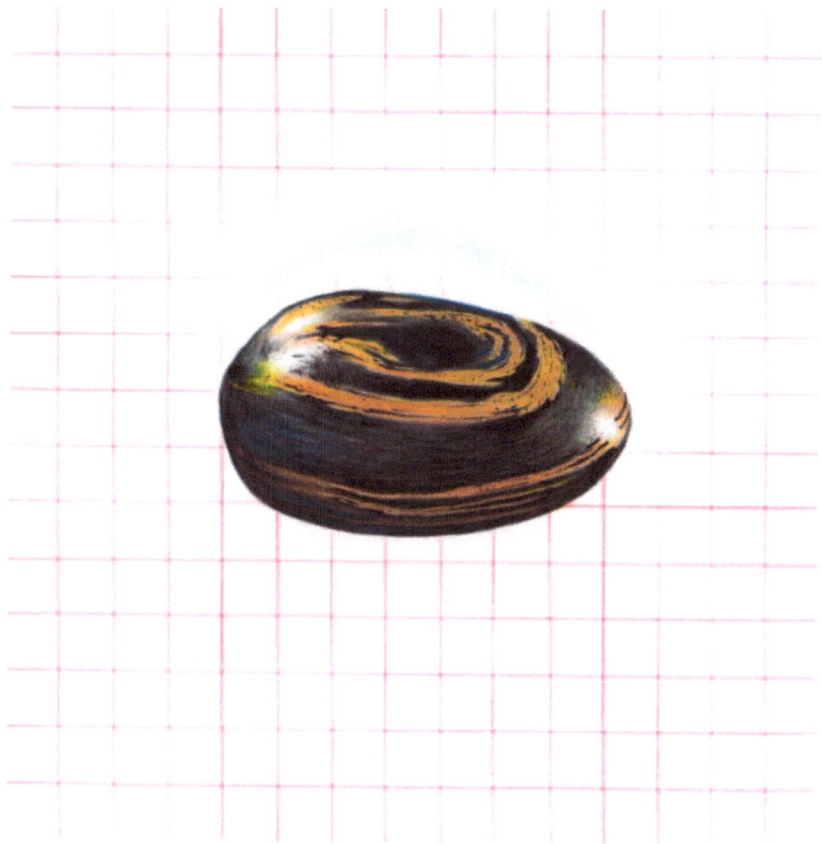

Seer Stone, 2015

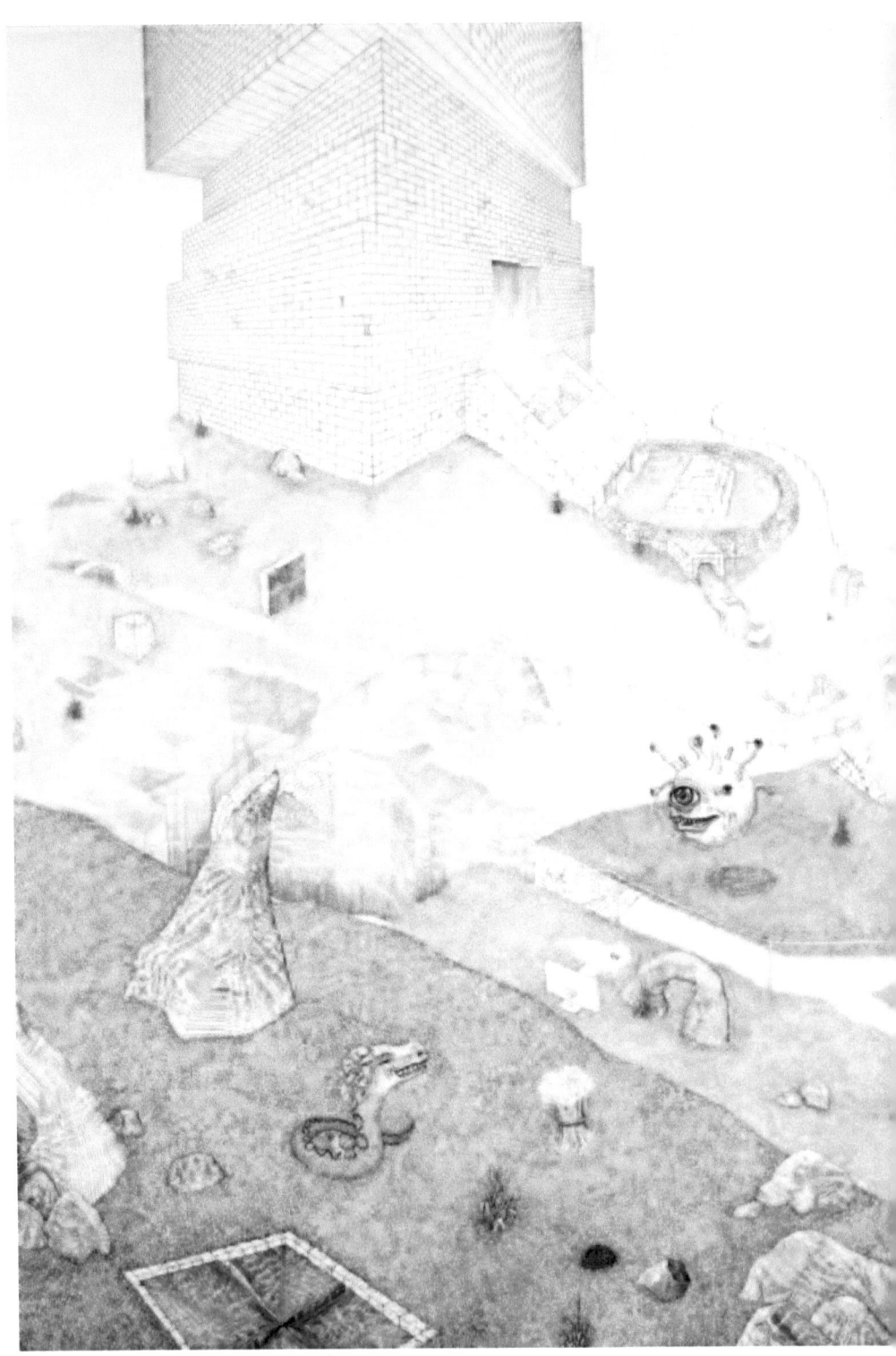

Lehi's Vision, 2010

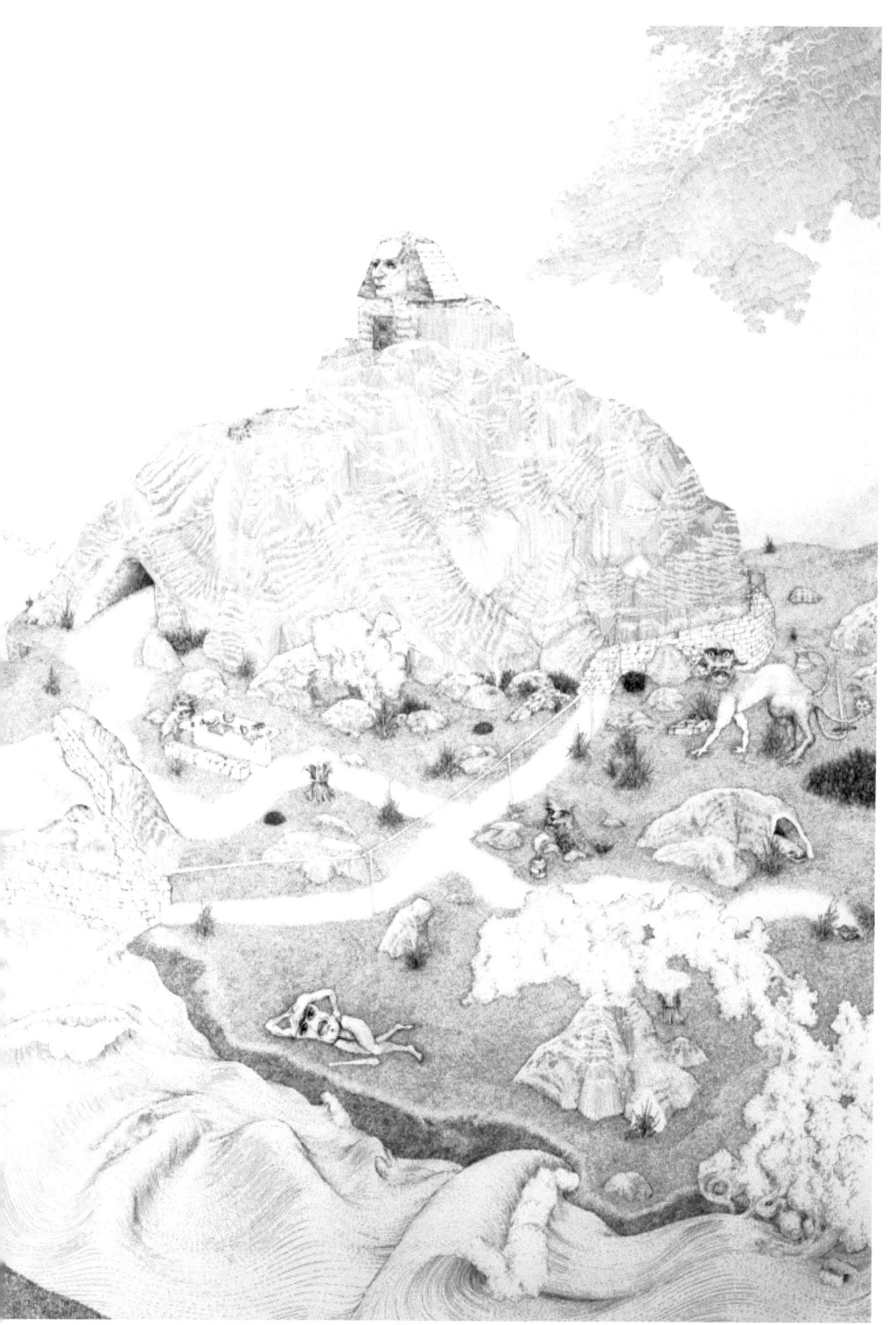

a dream about a great and spacious building, a field, a rod of iron, a fountain, etc. But that's not my question. I wonder whether you, as you're reading religious texts, imagine alternate landscapes for them.

Casey: Sometimes. Especially the landscapes that have to do with some kind of paradise, heaven, or Garden of Eden. Paradise to me has a lush, carpet-like grass on all surfaces. You can sit down and have a picnic any-where. And it's a dry, Western states grass that isn't crawling with bugs. And there are no muddy banks on rivers. Just grass all the way up to the babbling brooks. And more animals than humans. Lots of bears.

Glen: And secondly, tell me about your reaction to R. Crumb's illustrations for the *The Book of Genesis*, published in 2009. Is he an influence in your work?

Casey: He had a profound influence on me. I saw that work when it showed at the San Jose Museum of Art. I was floored by everything about it from his research, his respect for the material even though he is an athe-ist, his completely original figurative style, and the craft of his drawings. I remember seeing the whiteout halo he put around the Tree of Knowledge of Good & Evil so it would stand out from the background. And I felt vindi-cated that if someone like him, with his history in underground comics, could make work about religion, I certainly could.

Glen: When you finish a game, and you squeeze every possible reward out of it, and you get to the highest level or whatever the objective, do you ever go back to play it again? Or are you done with it and want to move on? And maybe this is an unfair comparison, but given the connec-tion between your work and games, when you finish a drawing, are you done with it, or do you want to go back and explore it again from a differ-ent angle—as an viewer?

Casey: I am very much done and want to move on with both. The tedium of making small, repetitive marks probably has something to do with it. But even in video games there is a pattern of combat that is tedious and be-gins to feel like work. I'm always excited to play that next game and fill that white void.

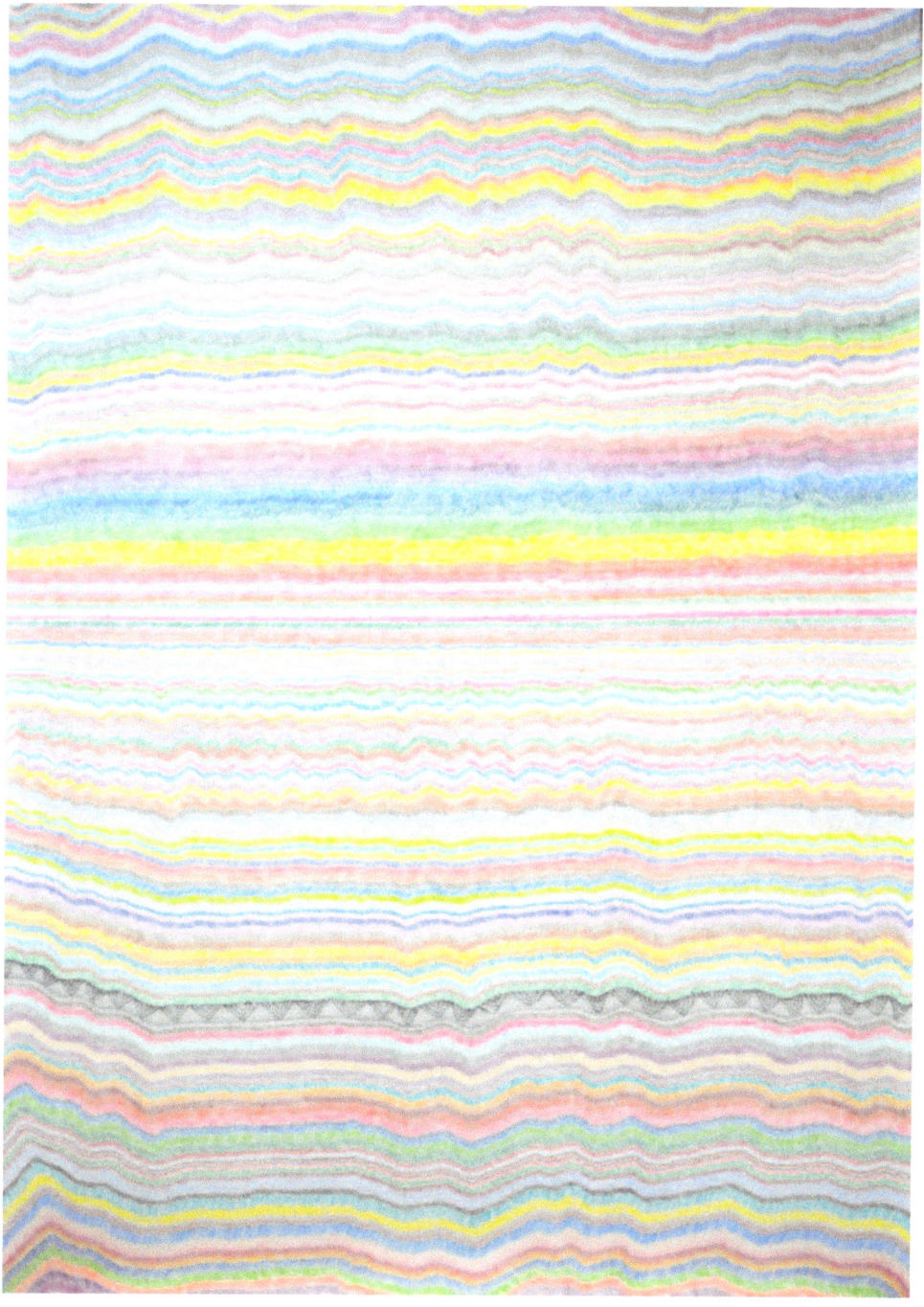

It Comes in Waves, 2012

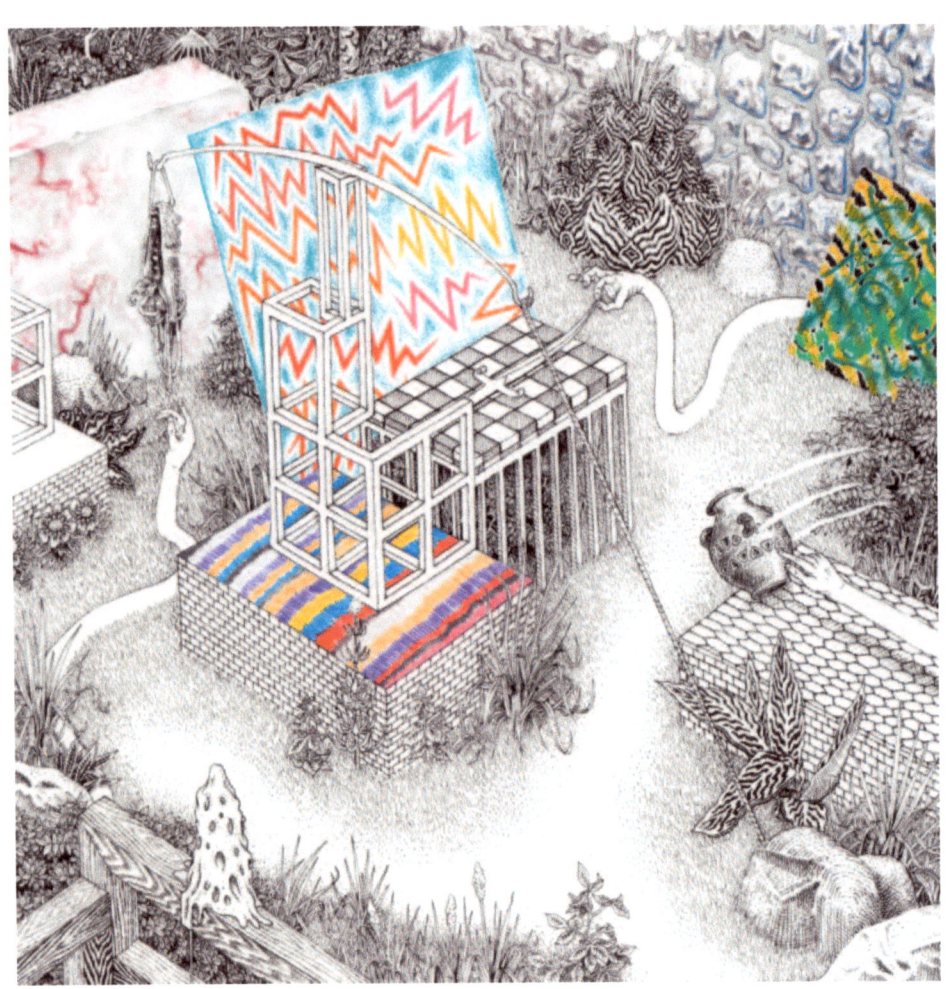

Grasping, 2015

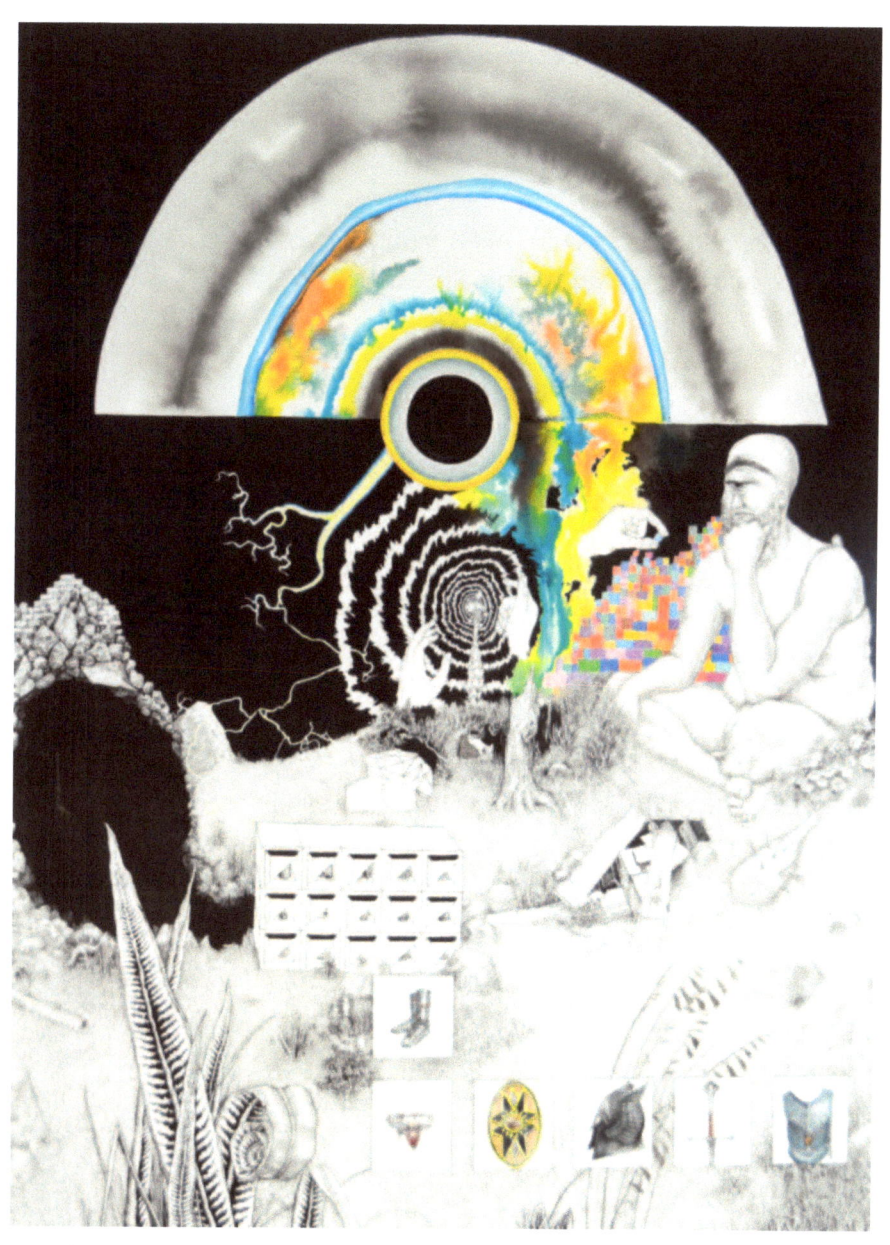

Cyclops, 2011

Casey Jex Smith (b. 1976) USA

M.F.A in Painting, San Francisco Art Institute, 2005
B.F.A. in Painting, Brigham Young University, 2003

Selection exhibitions:
Solo exhibitions
2015 Wars and Rumors of Wars, Writ & Vision, Provo, UT
2012 Fiend in the Void, Allegra LaViola Gallery, NYC
2012 Soul Flayer, Gallery 468, Provo, UT
2010 Doomslangers, Allegra LaViola Gallery, NYC
2009 Gird Your Elves and Be Broken in Pieces, LaViolaBank Gallery, NYC
2008 Matter Unorganized, Swarm Gallery, Oakland, CA
2008 New Work, Peter Miller Gallery, Chicago, IL
2007 There Is No End To Matter, Swarm Gallery, Oakland, CA
2006 New Work, Central Utah Art Center, Ephraim, UT
2003 Three Grids: Past, Past, Present, Provo Arts Council Gallery, Provo, UT

Two-person exhibitions
2014 Voices and Visions, Casey Jex Smith & Carrie Day, Launchpad Cooperative, Toledo, OH
2012 Glitter Guts, Gallery Protocol, Gainesville, FL
2010 Casey Jex Smith, John Casey, Galerie Polaris, Paris, France
2010 Stock Up on Heal and Mana Potions, Swarm Gallery, Oakland, CA
2006 Come, Come, Ye Saints! And Temple Bilds, Fifty50 Gallery, Chicago, Ill

Group exhibitions
2015 2, Good Mother Gallery, Oakland, CA
2015 Big Heads, Heroes, and Dancing Dogs, Texas Tech University, Lubbock, TX
2015 Pizza Party, Airlock Gallery, San Marcos, CA
2014 Under the Influence, Phillips, NYC
2014 Ducks, Curated by Ryan Travis Christian, Greenpoint Terminal Gallery, Brooklyn, NY
2014 New American Color, Curated by Jefferson Nelson, Dean & Sons Automotive, Toledo, OH
2013 Utah Biennial: Mondo Utah, Utah Museum of Contemporary Art, Salt Lake City, UT

2013 Tin, curated by Jared Lindsay Clark, Rio Gallery, Salt Lake City, UT

2012 We Could Be Heroes: The Mythology of Monsters and Heroes in Contemporary Art, Brigham Young University Museum of Art, Provo, UT

2012 Black Foliage, curated by Matthew Craven, Nudashank, Baltimore, MD

2012 Black Foliage, curated by Matthew Craven,48 Bowery, NYC

2012 Where My Cones At?, curated by Ryan Travis Christian, Double Break, San Diego, CA and POVevolving Gallery, LA, CA

2012 The Secret Decoder Ring, curated by Adam Bateman, HPGRP Gallery, NYC

2012 Patchbox, Cargo, Rome, Italy

2011 Drawing Now Paris with Galerie Polaris, Paris, France

2011 On Spirituality: Emerging Visions of the Spiritual, Gallery 842, Marshall University, Huntington, WV

2010 An Impossible Match, Galerie Polaris, Paris, France

2010 Phantasmorganica, Allegra LaViola Gallery, NYC

2010 Indulgences, Concertina Gallery at GOFFO @ NEXT, Chicago, ILL

2010 Friends of Friends, GARFO Art Center, Salt Lake City, UT

2009 Paper, Peter Miller Gallery, Chicago, ILL

2009 Regime Change, Swarm Gallery, Oakland, CA

2008 Selections Spring 2008, The Drawing Center, NYC

2008 microwave 6, Josee Bienvenu Gallery, NYC

2008 The Exquisite Line, Sherman Gallery, Boston University, Boston, MA

2008 The Brand New Deal, Caren Golden Fine Art, NYC

2008 Bring the Noise, WMFU Benefit, Printed Matter, NYC

2008 West, Wester, Westest, Fecal Face Dot Gallery, San Francisco, CA

2008 Freak of Nature, 111 Minna Gallery, San Francisco, CA

2008 Close Calls, Headlands Center for the Arts, Sausalito, CA

2007 Bliss, Roberts & Tilton, Los Angeles, CA

2007 The Total Power of Such a Signal Is Infinite, Okay Mountain, Austin, TX

2007 Three Solo Shows, ADA Gallery, Richmond, VA

2006 East Side Story, Yerba Buena Center for the Arts, San Francisco, CA

2006 Utopia, 111 Minna Gallery, San Francisco, CA

2006 Monster Drawing Rally, Southern Exposure, San Francisco, CA

2005 Pacific Lines, Yancey Richardson Gallery, NYC

2005 Lobot Retrospective, Lobot Gallery, Oakland, CA

2004 19th Annual Spiritual and Religious Art Exhibit, Springville Museum of Art, Springville, UT

2004 Paper Awesome!, Mimi Barr, San Francisco, CA

2004 L.P.'s, Provo Art Council Gallery, Provo, UT

2001 Minute: a boxed set of miniature multiples, Artists Space, NYC

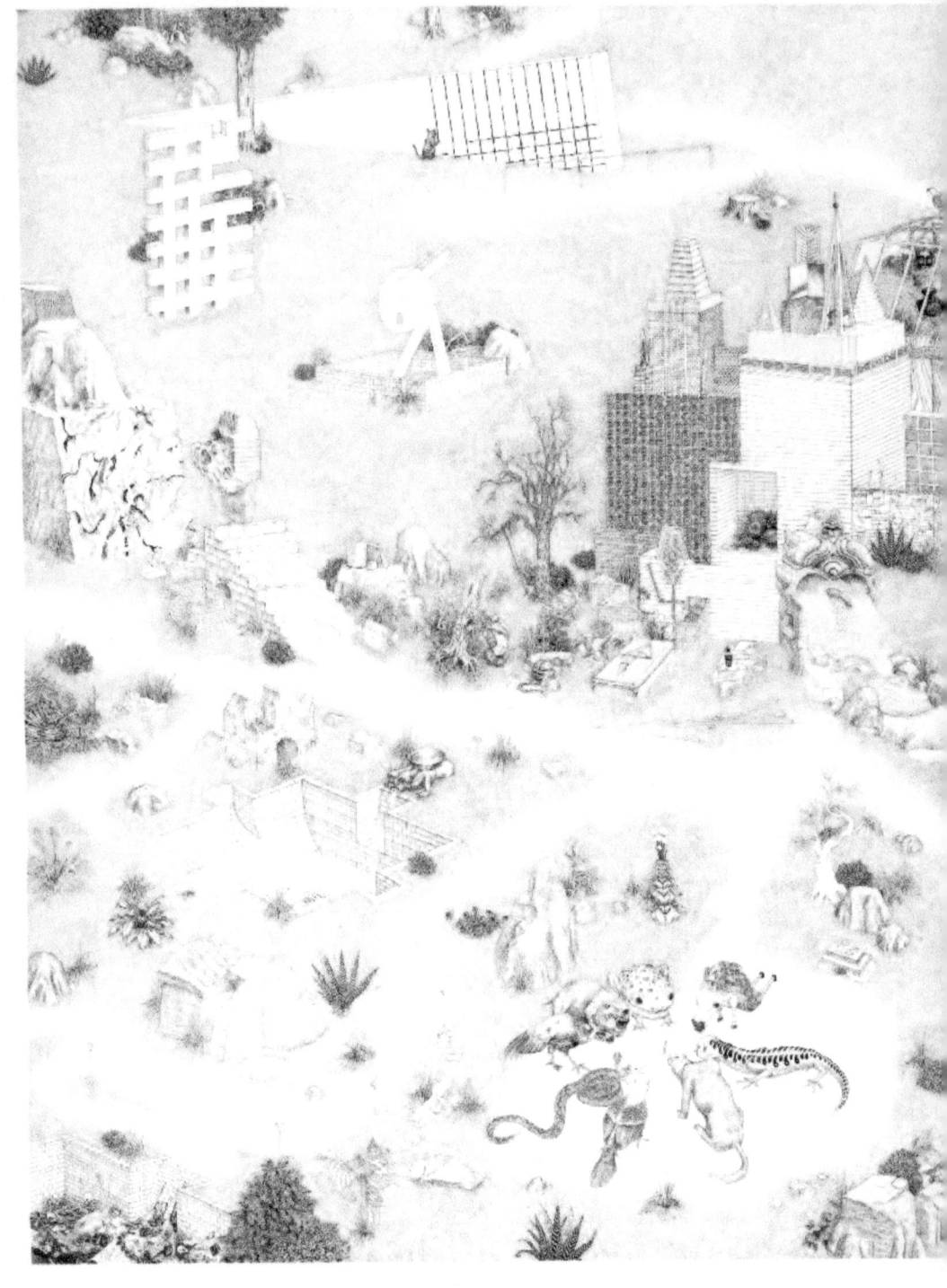

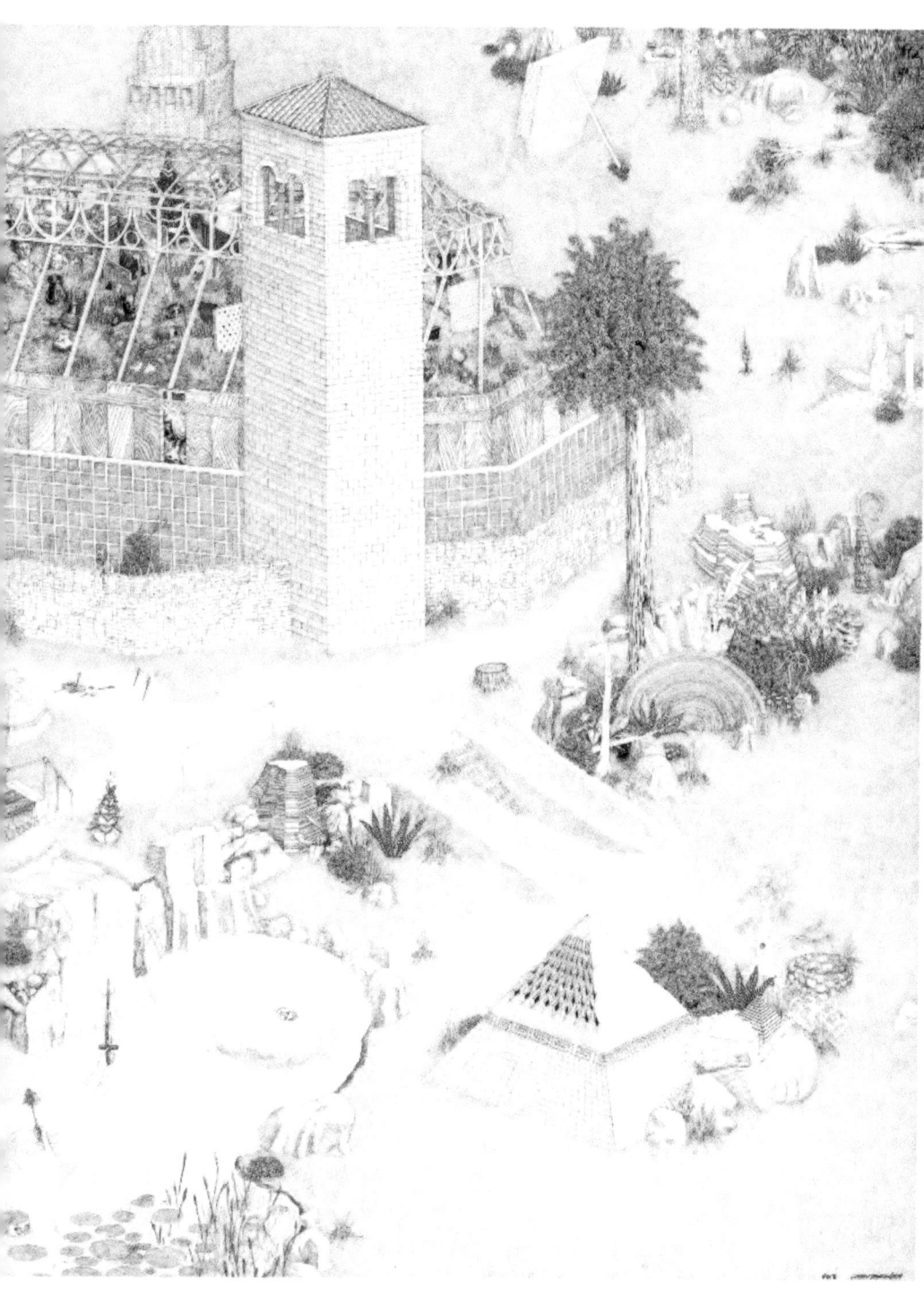

2013, 2013

Exhibition checklist

Limp, 2015
pen and colored pencil on paper
7.5 x 7.5 in.

Grasping, 2015
pen and colored pencil on paper
7.5 x 7.5 in

Vultures, 2014
pen on paper
7.5 x 7.5 in.

Pinch, 2015
pen, watercolor, and colored pencil on paper
9 x 9 in.

Seer Stone, 2015
colored pencil on paper
7.5 x 7.5 in

142 Painting Studies or Pries Spells, 2011
colored pencil, pencil, and pen on paper
22 x 22 in.

Churning, 2011
pen and watercolor on paper
20 x 18 in.

Finding Patterns, 2011
pen, colored pencil, and watercolor on paper
22 x 18 in.

Encumbered, 2010
pen & ink and watercolor on paper
19 x 19 in.

Cyclops, 2011
pen & ink and colored pencil on paper
30 x 22 in.

Stash, 2015
acrylic on canvas
24 x 24 in.

Lord Spelldyal 2012
pen on paper
10.5 x 7.5 in.

Loyal Udogold, 2012
pen on paper
10.5 x 7.5 in.

King Belian Shipsale, 2012
pen on paper
10.5 x 7.5 in.

It Comes in Waves, 2012
colored pencil and pen on paper
50 x 38 in.

Too Many Attacks to Count, 2012
colored pencil and spray paint on paper
50 x 38 in.

Sisyphean Shards, 2014
pen and colored pencil on paper
29 x 40 in.

2013, 2013
pen on paper
38 x 50 in.

Lehi's Vision, 2010
pen on paper
58 x 80 in.

Like Unto a Dish, 2013
pen on paper
10 x 8 in.

Sword of Laban +5 and Gear, 2010
colored pencil on paper
18 x 14 in.

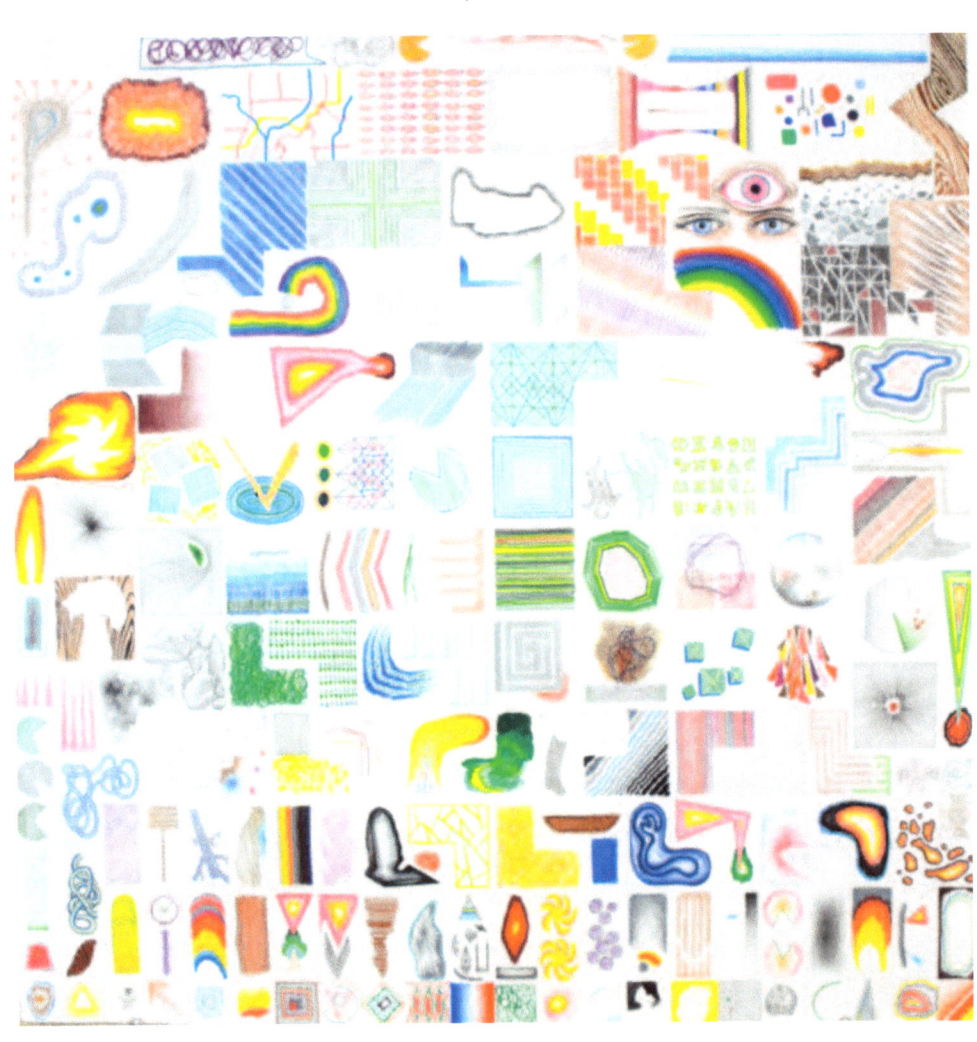

142 Painting Studies or Pries Spells, 2011